The tale of the old badger, the young fox and the wise owl

A short story and other bits and bobs
by Paul Gilbert

For the Moo and the Smidge with love

DEDICATION

To my great friends and mentors
Geoffrey Williams and Lawrence Smith
without whose care, faith and hard work
the LBC Wise Counsel story
would be nothing.

Braiswick
Felixstowe, Suffolk, England
http://www.braiswick.com

ISBN 978-09557008-8-0

British Library Cataloguing in
Publication Data available.

Cover by Oomph! Design
http://www.oomphdesign.co.uk

ACKNOWLEDGEMENTS

With grateful thanks to Tina Harris for collating, to Geoffrey Williams for editing and to Jon Honeyford for his great design work.

CONTENTS

Introduction

THE TALE OF THE OLD BADGER, THE YOUNG FOX AND THE WISE OWL

ARTICLES BY PAUL GILBERT

INTRODUCTION

This is my third volume of published articles following on from "Wise Counsel" in 2007 and "One Prick to Burst a Bubble" in 2009

I am always grateful for those who have been prepared to publish what I write and in since the year 2000 it is over one-hundred articles, and counting.

Many lawyers have taken issue with some of my more apocalyptic musings, but I have always written from a position of holding the profession in high regard and affection. Having predicted great change for many years it is a little odd to find this book being published at a time of very significant upheaval and change for the profession.

Running through all three books are the insights I believe can help individual lawyers make sense of a new order and I wish everyone well. As Darwin said; it is not the fittest of the species that survive, but the most adaptable to change.

All good wishes
Paul Gilbert

THE TALE OF THE OLD BADGER, THE YOUNG FOX AND THE WISE OWL

INTRODUCTION

Hi. My name is Paul and for a long time I have wanted to write a story about how we use our time, but I didn't have time to write it...

And you may ask "why bother" when bookstores the world over are full of eminent and worthy books on how to manage our time better. If you have managed to find the time to read any of them, then I should try to explain why I would like you to read this one too.

As I am someone who so singularly fails to manage his time very well, it is a subject that is very close to my heart.

This is a story that is therefore very personal and, I hope, more accessible for being so...it is also a story that I hope will settle in the minds not just of the high flyers and the high achievers, but also of those of us who walk in the foothills of ambition. I hope it might appeal to all ages from children at school with the huge demands that are now placed on their time to the older folks among us where time seems to fly so much more quickly than it has ever done before...

In this tale of the old badger, the young fox and the wise owl I am much more the old badger than either the young fox or the wise owl. Those who know me might think that I just have perpetrated an extraordinary understatement... How could I be anything else, of course I am the old badger!

However, knowing that I am the old badger might just add a little resonance to my words. As you will see I am clearly not preaching from any vantage point on this perennial issue. Life is very tough sometimes; work can be very tough as well - and achieving the right balance for ourselves and for all those we try to please is always going to be a work in progress, never a completed task.

So my first objective has been to write something that is less about the mechanics of managing time and more about the emotion of managing time.

In my opinion this is not something that should be written as if it could be reduced to a simple checklist or described as if it were as straightforward as any logical anodyne process...

Managing time for many people is so much more than this; it is in fact intrinsically tied into our character and our personality. Recognising this makes the issue more visceral, but probably harder to resolve. This is not, therefore, an "A, B, C..." guide to better time management, but more a gentle peeling back of something more fundamental and a little more revealing of our weaknesses as people. This is a tale about the nature of balance in the span of a whole career – whatever it is that we choose to do to make ends meet.

My second objective has been to ensure that anything I write on the subject of managing time should not waste the reader's time and so I have kept this very short.

I hope you might make a little time to read it; and I hope that when you have read it, you will not regret making that time...

CHAPTER ONE:
IN THE WOODS,
BUT NOT SEEING THE TREES

"I ache all over," said the old badger. "I ache so much, it hurts even to breathe."

"Oh dear," said the young fox. "Whatever have you done?"

"He has done nothing but work all his life," interrupted the wise owl. "He works so hard, every minute of every hour of every day, and when he has finished one task, he begins another. No time for rest, no time for play, just time for work."

"That's not entirely true," said the old badger grumpily. "I have had the odd quiet day - days when I could see the sky and when I could smell the grass; but it is just a fact of life these days for all of us, whoever we are, whatever we do…we are all so much busier than ever before."

"I don't want it to be a fact of my life," said the young fox, surprised that he had spoken out loud a thought that was in his head. "I don't want to be like you, old badger. I want to be able to chase my tail for fun, to play with my friends and to see my cubs. I want to do a good day's work for sure, but not to the exclusion of everything else."

"And that is what I wanted too," said the now even grumpier old badger. "I was just like you. No badger chooses to ache all over…no badger chooses to miss out on fun and family. I don't want this life, but this is my work, and this is what I must do to stay in my work. Every month is slightly busier than the one before and before you know it, before you can notice it, before you realise it, you wake up one day and you ache all over. It is not my choice, it is not my doing, it is just my life."

"That's not true," said the wise owl determinedly. "In reality you have chosen to ache all over, you have chosen to do more and more work and you have chosen not to see the sky or smell the grass, but it is not too late and you can still choose to have some fun."

"No I can't," said the old badger indignantly. "It isn't my fault; just look at my in-tray. I cannot possibly walk away from all that work. That is the trouble with all you wise owl types, chirping up from the safety of a high perch. You have no real understanding of my world and yet you feel you can dish out your "clever" banalities and your platitudinous homilies. No doubt you have a slogan or two as well, or a new three-letter acronym to remind me how clever you are and how unclever I am. Perhaps I should work "smarter" or strive for this or that; but, I'll have you know, I work very smartly; I am commended by all my colleagues and customers on how well I work. I am appreciated by them all for my dedication and my commitment. I have been promoted because of these things and I was awarded a "badger of the month" certificate for all my efforts too.

"I do not choose to ache all over; I choose to be professional, to have integrity, to be valued by my peers and my customers. I am a model worker."

The young fox looked a little sheepish (not an easy look for a young fox) and thought about chasing his tail.

The wise owl just looked a little wiser, to the obvious irritation of the old badger.

"And another thing," said the old badger, unsure now how he might put an end to his rant. "Every old badger I know is like me. We do not like the way it is, but we have a sense of duty; so please do not criticise me for doing the right thing; it is just a fact of life today."

"Is he right?" the young fox asked the wise owl, hoping the old badger was wrong, but fearing he might be right.

"There certainly are a lot of old badgers like him," said the wise owl calmly. "And to them it is perhaps a fact of their old badger lives. Nor is he wrong to say that he is valued by his colleagues and his customers, but we can all be liked for trying to please people. He is wrong, however, to think that it always has to be this way and he is certainly wrong to think that aching all over is either acceptable or inevitable."

"I don't want to ache all over," said the young fox. "What can I do so that I do not grow up to be like an old badger?"

"A very good question," said the wise owl. "I will tell you, but you will not listen, because young foxes never do."

"I am listening," said the young fox, chasing his tail.

"Umm," said the wise owl. "I don't think so, but I will tell you anyway. Being an old badger is a choice we make because we feel we do not have any other choices; what I will tell you is how we can reveal some new choices and how we can then make those new choices become real in our worlds."

"It will be more platitudinous nonsense," harrumphed the old badger. "I know it will...I really don't have time for this."

"Let the young fox make up his own mind," soothed the wise owl, unsurprised by the old badger's sceptical response. And then he placed in front of the young fox three small sticks, three small stones and three sea shells.

The young fox stopped chasing his tail and sat down looking a little bemused (a slightly easier look for a young fox than sheepish).

"Told you," huffed the old badger. "It is more nonsense from the house of the glib and the easy. Sticks, stones and sea shells? Pah! You can tell he has been to some fancy management school for this stuff - a school for those too clever to actually do a real job! He is taking you for a fool. The world is full of gurus pontificating short cuts to nowhere and peddling snake oil for the gullible."

The young fox, however, ignored the ranting old badger and looked intrigued (an even easier look for a young fox than bemused or sheepish) as he started to examine the small sticks, stones and sea shells.

"What do they mean?" he asked the wise owl. "I don't want a short cut, or snake oil...I really don't...but I do want to know that the old badger's way is not the only way."

"Then listen very carefully," said the wise owl. "These things I have given you, the small sticks, the stones and the sea shells, are not important in themselves; like all metaphors, slogans, ideas, templates and tools of any description, they can only work if two things happen; first they must strike a chord within you and second you must be prepared to make a change to the way you do things as a result."

"I am listening," said the young fox.

"Then let me explain what they mean," said the wise owl.

CHAPTER TWO:
THE STICKS, THE STONES
AND THE SHELLS OF OUR LIVES

"The three small sticks represent three things that you must always remember about the constraints of time.

"I have chosen sticks because they were once part of magnificent living trees, but now, separated from their trees, they are brittle and not nearly as amazing as they once were. We must not allow ourselves to become separated from our friends and family trees by just working longer and longer hours:

For the first small stick, remember that there will always be more things to do in the day than the time you have to do them in. You must realise therefore that simply working longer and longer hours does not solve this problem, but it might create other problems.

For the second small stick, remember that the better you become at your job then the more demands there will be on your time from customers and colleagues who want your help and support. You must realise therefore that simply working longer and longer hours does not solve this problem, but it might create other problems.

For the third small stick, remember that managing your relationships with customers and colleagues is not about trying to please them as an end in itself; it is about doing the right things, doing them in the right way and doing them at the right time. You must realise therefore that simply working longer and longer hours does not solve this problem, but it might create other problems.

"We talk about "making time", but we cannot actually make time; what we mean to do is to prioritise tasks and time to make the best use of our time. In this way time is like a magic rucksack where there always seems to be another space we can find to put something in, but only if we have planned to pack what we need to take, to balance the heavy and the light and to be thoughtful about what goes in and in what order.

"The three sticks remind us that time is something we have to manage and to take control of and that we also have to live in the moment to make the most of the moment.

"The three small stones represent three things you must never compromise, because they are fundamentally about your values and the things that you would like to endure in the hearts of others when they think of you.

"I have chosen stones because they are the hard, irreducible core of what we stand for; they are the foundation on which we build our character:

For the first small stone, remember that doing a less good job than you are capable of doing diminishes you and makes you a smaller fox; it will not only make you less valued and less valuable, but it will also sap your self-confidence and your self-belief. It is the most destructive cycle of all. Do not fear being stretched; reach out and others will reach out to you.

For the second small stone, remember that blaming systems or customers or policies or colleagues or equipment changes absolutely nothing. Waiting for things to get better is like waiting for someone else to carry you because you cannot be bothered to take the first steps. In the end things change through how we behave, how we influence and what we do with what we have. Encourage in yourself an attitude that values seeing the potential to improve things rather than an attitude to criticise the weaknesses and failings of others. If your engagement is unconditional, progress can be made.

For the third small stone, remember that doing nothing when you could do something abdicates responsibility and allows sloth and ineptitude to fill the space you vacate. Improving the way we work is about taking action, not suffering inaction. If we have the talent, the patience and the will to tolerate inconvenience and inefficiency, we also have an equal amount of talent to invent, innovate and inspire. Never choose to stand still when you can take

a step forward.

"Keep these small stones with you and rely on their strength to keep you strong.

"The three small sea shells represent three things we must always strive to do; these are the keys to unlocking a better way, but like sea shells they are delicate and will turn to sand if they are crushed by pounding waves.

"You must therefore protect them as well as remember what they stand for:

For the first small sea shell, remember to treat your time as a precious thing to be shared with friends, family and work. We plan our work lives within our diaries, our computers, our Blackberries and our staff; every moment is assigned and aligned; and yet friends and family are often left with the dregs of our day. So plan the whole day for the wholeness we need in our lives.

For the second small sea shell, remember to constantly assess and reassess the value you achieve for the time you invest. Everything we do can be done better and not everything we do adds enough value for the time it takes. Do not let bad habits slow you down, silting up your effectiveness. Did you know that, over a year, if you could save just five percent of the time it takes you to complete your tasks, then you will have found the equivalent of an additional ten working days - ten days perhaps to reinvest in your family or friends?

For the third small sea shell, remember that we are all creatures that need praise and sometimes we allow ourselves to follow that praise instead of creating new praiseworthy things for people to appreciate about our contribution. If people see that we work long hours and praise us for doing so, we will often repeat this behaviour to receive that praise again. Soon we can become trapped - so heavily reliant on working long hours that the only thing people will see to praise is the hours we work. You must therefore build relationships with colleagues and customers to ensure that our value is seen not just in long hours, but in all sorts of things - in our results, efficiency, effectiveness, acumen, timeliness, humour, empathy, trustworthiness, thoughtfulness and leadership.

"There…so what do you think of that?"

The young fox paused, picking up the sticks, stones and sea shells and looking at each with thoughtful care.

"That's a lot to take in; I wonder what it really all means?" he asked himself hesitantly.

"I don't have time for all this nonsense," said the old badger, and he sloped off to a predictably difficult future, eyes weighed down by the heaviest of frowns, aching all over and failing to see the sky or to smell the grass on his way.

The young fox looked up. He wanted to say something to the old badger; he didn't want the old badger to think he had got it wrong or wasn't valued or respected, but the old badger had gone.

"What does it all mean?" the young fox asked the wise owl.

The wise owl looked away at the old badger and sighed a little sadly.

"It means," he said, turning back his gaze to the young fox, "that you really do have choices and the choices are real, but they are not choices I can make for you. They are choices that only you can make."

CHAPTER THREE:
ENDING THE BEGINNING

This is not a story that has an easy end. In every wood we will meet old badgers; they work hard and they have much to offer; but it is often delivered at a personal cost to themselves and one that they realise only when it is too late.

Managing time is not just about the tasks for the day; managing time is about looking at the span of a career. Trying to get the balance right in this dimension, for colleagues, for our employers, for our families and for ourselves is one of the very hardest things of all.

We may think that the ways of the old badgers are outdated and that their lives are less fulfilled; we may even think they are stubborn and wrong, but they should not be shunned, pitied or lectured. Old badgers in many organisations are often the link between what the office manual says is in theory the way things should be done and the real life experience of how things get done in practice.

They help to make things work, they are productive and they are often loyal and steadfast to a fault; which then makes the disappointment they feel when their contribution is suddenly less valued all the more poignant and hard for them to understand.

Old badgers are therefore vulnerable because, when the young foxes arrive, their ways are often seen as old ways and, for young foxes, old ways are rarely seen as good ways.

It is easy to dismiss and alienate the old badgers by foisting on them new processes, new technology and new three letter acronyms, in part knowing that we are only setting them up to fail.

So while we may not want to be old badgers ourselves, we should still value at least some of their ways.

In our own worlds this tale is a timeless story of juggling priorities, but it also has a further context, that of one generation passing control to another and of our ever moving place in that transition.

My hope is that we will not just seek the ever more efficient prioritisation of the day to day; my hope is actually much more about understanding that in work we must try to attain a balance that encourages new ideas, but which does not dismiss past experiences and that in doing so we must also, crucially and fundamentally, find the right balance between what we value in work and what we value outside work.

Not all old badger ways are bad or inefficient ways.

Not all the energy and enthusiasm of young foxes is well directed (sometimes not even well intentioned).

We all need to feel valued.

We all need to make a contribution of value.

We all should look to improve our contribution as much as our abilities allow.

Above all, we should occasionally pause to look at the sky, smell the grass and reflect on our own personal small sticks, stones and sea shells.

The end

ARTICLES BY PAUL GILBERT

SHALL WE COMPLY
WITH THE LAW?

The Compliance team is often seen as the poor relation to the in-house legal team in a business; but I suspect this is all about to change.

Imagine asking any Board director "Would you please specify the laws and regulations that apply to your business that you will be choosing not to comply with in future?" The answer, of course, will be an incredulous "No". It is the shortest answer any question can have, but this "No" is packed with consequences.

First and obviously it indicates that the Board expects to comply with all applicable laws and regulations. This must be the position of all Boards and a completely uncontroversial statement; but if this is the case then all Boards must also be interested to understand:

- What exactly are the applicable laws and regulations in every jurisdiction in which we trade?
- How do those laws and regulations apply to our business?
- How do we track how any new laws will impact our business?
- How do we then comply with all these laws in a way that is proportionate to the risk, but which is also assuredly within the law?
- Then, how do we know we are actually complying with these laws so that we have the evidence to back up our desire to comply? And finally
- What do we do if we sense that we are not complying and what do we do when we find out that we are definitely not complying?

And so for any significant and mature business the Compliance function is born.

In-house legal teams might once have been a little sniffy about compliance work; it was, after all, for the "box tickers" down the corridor; but in fact Compliance is of far more interest to a Board than most of the work a legal department undertakes. It is directly relevant to the duties of directors, goes to the heart of personal and corporate reputation and is always on the formal business agendas.

It is very hard to outsource Compliance and not lose empathy and proportionality. In addition a compliance failure will often be brought to the attention of a regulator and this in turn can impact reputational risk, the ability to trade as well as having financial penalties. In extreme circumstances directors may even face personal sanctions in a way that most legal work does not entail.

Whereas nearly all legal work can be outsourced and in any event does not usually impact every policy, process and person in the business. Legal work, in this context, is frankly not that significant. Indeed I will go so far as to say that if in-house teams do not embrace Compliance and bring to it all their creativity and expertise, then they are putting at risk their own value to their businesses and missing a significant opportunity to become strategically important.

The opportunity to do so however is very much alive. This is not a closed shop and there is much work to be done for lawyers and compliance professionals alike. For many organisations Compliance is something of a mystery, while for others it is very much a maturing function. The Compliance journey has really only just begun.

It would be easy to make Compliance bureaucratic, insensitive to business priorities and superficial. Not only should it be the opposite of these failings, it should also encourage better risk management, help to raise standards in the conduct of business and mitigate the consequences of any failings that are probably inevitable in any large scale operation.

Importantly businesses must also come to appreciate that they have a duty of care to help all their employees avoid the consequences of inadvertent breaches of rules and regulations. In this context if a company is true to its values then it will invest in ensuring compliance requirements and responsibilities are evident in the recruitment process, induction, training and appraisal. Compliance is part of everything.

Compliance might not be sexy in the way that that some lawyers think an M&A deal sets the pulse racing or a high profile dispute plays out in the courts, but it is an essential assurance function and a crucial link in the governance chain. Indeed it is one of the few areas that provides everyone from Board member to the lowest operational grade with a common objective.

Legal work will continue to be important (obviously) and if it is done well it will always be of significant value; Compliance however can be and should be part of the DNA of a business. It is an unsung function, but one that I predict will become increasingly significant, increasingly valuable and increasingly strategic.

External advisors and in-house lawyers look out; this may be your best opportunity to make a very big difference to your business; so don't be sniffy about it and don't leave it to the box tickers!

A LITTLE LESSON
ABOUT A BAG...

...Sometimes I just sit; sometimes I just sit and watch.

A few days back I was able to observe a small moment in someone's life. They were holding a bag of shopping, not a "bag-for-life" but the flimsiest of plastic carrier bags. It was bulging with probably too many things and sure enough the bag split and the contents were strewn across the pavement.

The hapless bag carrier looked forlornly at the hole in her now useless bag and set about picking up the packets of food, bottles of water, magazines etc. She soon realised however that she could not pick up everything and still hold it all in her hands ...and you could see the sense of resignation and despair in her face.

People passed her on the pavement; some offered a sympathetic word, one or two picked things up for her, but this was not going to help her much; unless she had another means to carry her shopping home – she was more than a bit stuck.

I then noticed this old chap come up to her with a couple of new empty bags. He had evidently seen her predicament, popped into the shop she had been in and came out with two new bags.

I liked this alot...I liked the "don't wait to be asked" attitude, I liked the practicality and the simplicity of the help and I liked the lack of drama about it all.

At this point, you may be relieved to know, I am not going to do some cheesy segue into client care and relationship management. I reckon you were there before me and all set to huff out loud at another sugared cliché.

No, this is not a metaphor for client service, but something deeper.

In a real client situation the ultimate goal is obviously to send the client an invoice and get paid. In effect, by analogy, my old chap having rescued the shopping situation would now ask the shopper for some money and she thrilled by his help would then willingly pay.

And here you can see how the analogy breaks down; if the old chap had asked for money it would feel really shabby and it would also undo all the goodwill immediately.

The story therefore is not about how client service wins the day; client service builds goodwill, but may not have immediate financial returns.

This analysis however is a bit dull, because clearly businesses have to make money. Can we therefore make money from this situation? The answer is "not very easily", but stay with me as I extend the analogy further and suggest four different strategies...

Option one: We could set up a pavement stall outside the shop selling robust shopping bags. We might get a reasonable passing trade and if we could offer cashiers an "inducement" to overfill their flimsy bags this might pay dividends too!

The essence of this option however is a short term gain with an uncertain business plan and low growth potential. To really make money we need to go to the shop-owners with a solution and in this way we might be able to achieve an income that is more sustainable and scalable.

Option two: We go to the shop-owners with a training proposition to train the cashiers not to overfill their flimsy bags. This however only gives us a one-off fee and clearly no profit for the shop-owners.

Option three: We go to the shop-owners with a "bag for life solution". Here there is an opportunity to profit share with them and make an easy early profit; but once everyone has their bag, sales will predictably fall.

Option four: What if we could create not just a bag for life, but something extra as well? Then we might create sustainable and scalable profit. For example, what if the bag had a seasonal motif (spring, summer, etc) or different designs of another sort and shoppers could trade in their old bag for a new one for a fraction of the cost of a new bag. In effect we have developed a market for selling bags and also a market for exchanging bags. If we then sell the second-hand bags to local market stalls we have a derivative market to profit from as well.

So what are the lessons for lawyers?

1. Looking after the shopper, like my old chap did at the start, is important to demonstrate what you stand for, in effect your brand values. It shows the type of people you are and how credible you will be in other situations; but it won't of itself make you money.

2. To create a sustainable business with a plan for growth you have to go back to proactively solving the problem, not reactively managing the symptoms. A problem for which you have the solution is potentially income for the longer term; managing symptoms is short term and unpredictable

3. To be truly successful for the long term however you must not just solve a problem, but add real value beyond the issue itself. You will need to be genuinely innovative, use your resources really well and segment your markets to leverage the maximum value you can from your expertise.

I wonder what you will see the next time you get a chance to just sit and watch.

"I'M NO JUDGE..."

In the summer of 1981 I worked on a building site. It was the summer of Botham's Ashes and Lady Di's wedding; of bad hair, big shoulders and terrible music. But the weather was wonderful and in my small corner of the world there was some great lads, great banter, huge mugs of tea, the Sun newspaper, and endless ribbing about me being a law student...you can imagine how it was. I lived the cliché for a few weeks and loved it...

Then one Friday afternoon the foreman asked me how much overtime I had done that week. I said "none" and he said, "I'll put you down for ten hours".

I cannot remember what I said, but I remember feeling very uncomfortable. I mentioned it to a mate and he just said "great, drinks are on you!"

My dad said that either I should go with it as I was part of the team or I should leave, but I definitely should not tell the boss. I took the extra money that week, but the next time it happened a couple of weeks later my unease was greater still and I walked off the site.

Why mention it? Because I really do not like the way we are demonising sections of the society we live in. The aggressive name calling, stigmatising and judging of people be they so called "scroungers", illegal immigrants, policeman on the take or phone hacking journalists...It makes me feel deeply uncomfortable.

Let me be clear I do not have any sympathy with excessive and systematic abuse of trust. If people have suffered that must be acknowledged; but I have a lot of sympathy for people who work in an environment where low level criminal activity has been tolerated, even encouraged, for years and where no-one seems to be harmed.

It is wrong, of course, and I am not saying it is right or a good thing. I am just saying I can see how it happens and, frankly, how it could so easily have been me.

What if there had been a whistleblower in 1981. What if my site team were set up by the manager and as the foremen finished the fraudulent return so several police officers came crashing into the huts and arrested us all.

In that first week I would have been guilty as hell and bang to rights. I might then have had a criminal record and I might never have become a lawyer. At that point, and trying not to sound melodramatic, my life might have been destroyed.

I knew then in my heart of hearts what was right and what was wrong and I tried to deal with it in my way.

I also knew what great lads I was working with and what a special team they were. They taught me so much about people and I can remember many more things I learnt on that building site than I can remember about any law lecture I attended that year. They worked hard and were good people.

However, like I say, I don't want to seem like I am condoning criminal behaviour, I just want some perspective and judgment to be applied.

Right now it is very likely that some police officers will lose their livelihoods for being too close to a journalist and journalists might lose their livelihoods for listening to a celebrity's phone messages. If you have ever lost a job you will know that this can be completely devastating. Some people never recover from it. Are we really saying in the cold light of day that the behaviour we are discussing is so rotten, so impossible to accept and so unforgiveable that we have to criminalise otherwise good people and punish them and their families?

I'm not sure I want to be part of that.

Our prime minister, it is said, was once part of a student "gang" that trashed the odd bar. The next day cash would have to exchange hands to make up for some of the loss and inconvenience. The behaviour was probably criminal, but I really wouldn't want him (even him) to have had his life blighted by his stupidity and thoughtlessness.

I think we are losing a sense of proportion. I think we are losing the ability to sanction in a way that acknowledges wrongdoing, but which also allows for reparation and for forgiveness.

And I really do not like the sanctimonious preaching from some quarters wielding the stick of twenty-twenty hindsight. You were not there, you do not know how it was; while you are entitled to your point of view, please do not point it at me. Besides, I was always taught that it was very poor manners to stand and point.

So, I am only speaking for myself, but with my criminal past in mind, who am I to judge? And who are you?

"EXTREME INERTIA" WHY CHANGE IF NOTHING'S ON FIRE?

It is often said that we only really contemplate change when there is a "burning platform"; in other words when the motivation for change is so pressing that we are in immediate peril or at the very least the status quo has become deeply, deeply unattractive.

We are generally very good at passively resisting change. In effect we have become expert in the art of practicing extreme inertia.

Extreme inertia is part of everyday life. How many of us wait until we have a wet sock before we fix the hole in our shoe, or have a tooth ache before we fix a broken tooth? In a less flippant example I once worked with an in-house team who told me their manager was rubbish, their business uninspiring and their colleagues stupid. When I pointed out that maybe they should change their outlook or leave nearly all the lawyers said in terms "well, better the devil you know"!

It seems clear to me that without the pressing motivation of pain/disadvantage, a situation that is obviously becoming unattractive or unpromising will still not be enough to make us change. I am convinced this is one reason why the legal profession isn't more excitable just now around all the things happening in our markets with new competitors, new regulation and different client expectations.

The men and women in our bigger law firms, for example, are well paid, work in nice offices and with intelligent colleagues. There is nothing much wrong here and perhaps therefore rather obviously no-one is jumping up and down for change. Indeed the perception for many is that while business might be a bit ropey just now, if you can stick it out and make it to partner, then more money and status is just around the corner.

Saying to anyone in this situation that the world is changing fast and you need to change with it, is counter intuitive. In addition the leadership in the profession, almost by definition, is at the top and reaping the benefits of the journey they have been on; the last thing they want is significant change while they are still at the helm.

There are therefore two possibilities to contemplate:

- First, that those who are calling for change to respond to a new emerging landscape are just plain wrong. Recessions come and go, markets bubble and burst, but in the end, lawyers are on safe ground longer term. Or
- The profession really is going through a major process of change, but that the negative consequences are not being fully felt so without the burning platform we are drifting on our raft of extreme inertia towards an unhappy end.

My view, for what it is worth, is that the legal market is in the throes of deep and dramatic change facilitated by technology, by liberalisation of markets and by different client expectations; but above all fuelled by a dawning realisation that being a "lawyer" doesn't mean very much if 60-80% of one's workload is process driven, administrative and largely routine.

There isn't a burning platform, not yet anyway, in part because clients do not fully realise the power they now have to effect significant change. The law firm response so far has been limited and when clients do force further changer the platform may start to smoulder if not actually catch fire.

What's to be done therefore?

My advice – and it is advice which should be comfortable even if you think I am wrong about the way the market is changing – is for firms to do three things:

1. Law firms should create a small project group (not all drawn from the senior ranks) to survey the market, sense check client ambition for change and to highlight risk and opportunity. The project group should report quarterly for the first year, but the ambition for the group should be to come forward with ideas that can be debated by the whole firm after a year of research.

2. Law firms should invite their trainee cohort and junior associates to come up with their ideas for what the firm might be like in five and ten years time in terms of the type of work the firm will it be doing, how will it deliver its services, what will be the profile of the client base etc. This review work should be done annually and should feed into both the project group and the senior management team

3. Firms must also engage with clients. Not necessarily to ask what they want (the Henry Ford observation is ever relevant "before the invention of the automobile, if you asked what folks wanted from transportation, they would have said faster horses") but to properly listen to their frustrations, concerns, their hopes, their ambitions etc and to then respond with service and product development.

The clever and important thing however is then to link all three activities, so that the outputs are brought together to be assessed, analysed and prioritised as part of a coherent effort to encourage adaption (at least) and possibly significant change.

The energy from these efforts might allow early detection of any "smoke" and give some focus and ambition to manage change more successfully than might be the case otherwise.

IN-HOUSE LAWYERS – A STRATEGIC ROLE FOR THE PROFESSION

In-house lawyers in the UK are the best in the world. No other sector of the legal profession delivers more value to business, more consistently and more innovatively than in-house lawyers and the General Counsel who lead the in-house teams are some of the most entrepreneurial and thoughtful leaders of lawyers in the world.

The US is often held up as the exemplar for in-house practice, but their legal market is less innovative and more restricted, while law firms are more powerful and companies more cautious. Elsewhere in Europe, and further afield in Africa and Asia, the in-house role is sometimes less well understood, is often still maturing and in some cases is not fully recognised by their country Law Societies and Bars.

In the UK however the Law Society fully recognises the value and importance of the profession's in-house community. The legal market here is also highly developed and a world centre. Companies based here who employ in-house lawyers can recruit from the best firms in the world and the lawyers that rise to the top in these companies combine not just great legal skills, but commercial skills, great leadership credentials and business acumen.

For the last twelve years I have been fortunate enough to work with some of the most talented in-house teams in the UK and globally and in my judgement the role of the in-house lawyer has never been more important and the talent more impressive.

However there is SO much more that needs to be done.

Most city law firms, notwithstanding their impressive glass towers and their global presence, are still stuck with a largely outdated model of service delivery and pricing. The top firms may be stock full of brilliant minds, but for the most part law firms frustrate. They are machines built to make money for partners and only reluctantly invest in innovation or diversification. In-house teams therefore have to become more demanding, but this is not about posturing for lower fees (leave this to procurement professionals) it is about partnering with their key legal services suppliers to drive long term innovation and investment in sustainable change.

This is really important because only General Counsel can fully appreciate what their businesses need from lawyers, how legal services should be developed, how risk management strategies and processes should filter and facilitate business decisions and how competitive advantage requires the fluid combination of accessibility, speed, judgement and wisdom.

The challenge for General Counsel in the UK is therefore not the challenge of many in-house lawyers around the world. Here they do not have to fight for a voice, to be seen as independent or risk being chronically under-resourced for the risks their businesses run.

In the UK General Counsel have a different challenge; it is the challenge of making a once-in-a-generation shift that will change the profession forever and have repercussions, done well, for legal services around the world.

Businesses need legal services that are designed to make business better, not lawyers richer. This means legal services (including advice, know-how, training, tools, systems and processes) that are available when needed, in a format and through channels that best suit each situation and at a price that is proportionate, transparent, reasonable and for value.

This will not be achieved however by posturing for change or asserting demands like a four-year old child in a toy shop. General Counsel have got to step up and change the game; they have go to work closely with their chosen law firms, insist that all self-interest is put aside and commit to a two to three year horizon that will see investment in systems, processes and people. In effect to build partnerships that ensure the very best of what in-house teams offer is seamlessly configured with the best of what law firms offer.

According to the Law Society there are 11000 in-house solicitors working in commercial and industrial organisations in England and Wales and a further 4000 in Local Government. Around 80000 work in private practice. So, very nearly 20% of the profession is not in private practice. If one-in-five lawyers are in in-house roles this means they are not just a significant constituency of legal advisors in their own right, but because they largely appoint the law firms their companies use, they are the biggest purchasers of legal services as well.

The time has come for General Counsel to be the architects of new services and new models for the delivery of those services; not the tenants in a world built by the law firms.

Given the excellent standing of the most senior lawyers in the most important in-house roles, this generation of General Counsel now carries the responsibility to help build a future that is good for business and good for the long term sustainability of the legal profession.

KNOWLEDGE AND WISDOM

I know something you don't know; if I share it with you, I will ask you to pay for it.

I am guessing this doesn't sound like a compelling proposition; indeed you might tell me where to put "it" and I am also guessing it might be somewhere where the sun don't shine.

...Even if you were minded to hear more you would want to better understand why it might be valuable to you before you paid anything; and you would probably suggest paying something only if the true value was fully revealed.

And yet the "I know something you don't know; if I share it with you, I will ask you to pay for it..." approach is a model for charging for legal services that is still commonplace today.

It always felt anachronistic to me and I never liked it, but the prevailing attitude appeared to be that anything else would work less well. In recent years however things have changed a lot. We are still nowhere near value-billing and even so called "innovative pricing" (always asked for in every panel review pitch) induces eye-rolling and hand-wringing in equal measure; even so a great deal has changed.

Take just one example, as we know there is a trend for certain types of legal work to strip-out individual lawyer time and to replace this with process and paralegals to drive the cost down.

For the right kind of work this is exactly what should happen and it is impressive to see it in operation. The approach sees law firms managing risk through efficient process, sending high volumes through the machine and making their profit from lower margins, but increased capacity. The lessons being learnt in this space however are also being applied to increasingly complex transactions/ litigation. Again I think this is a very good thing.

Better cost management is a key part of value and anyone who has spent any time in a non law firm environment is familiar with the annual edicts from on high – put in a process where there isn't one; then drive down costs within the process; finally never spend money that doesn't have to be spent.

In this regard law firms still have a long way to go; nearly all legal work has a significant administrative element and change is therefore long overdue to put in place process and to drive out cost...But value is never as simple as this and I am very concerned that in the rush to reduce costs and to commoditise legal work, we are mismanaging perceptions of what value means.

Not everything is just process, administrative or routine.

Lawyers must of course drive out unnecessary cost, but over time this will become an expected norm. What is now also needed is a sense of what is valued by clients and what is not valued by clients.

The distinction I would like to see drawn therefore is between information, which I believe carries much less value than ever before, and wisdom which I believe we do not value enough

Indeed in my view law firms must quickly appreciate that in order to secure profitable work (and not chase the price to the bottom of the market) they must learn to give away much more. They should give away precedents, templates, checklists, case notes...in fact anything that can be described as information.

On the other hand they should be properly rewarded for

insight and wisdom. Insight and wisdom is where the client can better manage risk, more fully appreciate opportunity, and perhaps even find competitive advantage. A few words of wisdom might save or make fortunes – and should be paid for accordingly.

Yet we are often stuck with the same time-based charges for some work that clients increasingly feel should carry minimal cost (or no cost at all) and for other work which they would be prepared to pay a fee linked to value.

This failure to differentiate is plain daft; it represents a systemic failure in our legal profession and makes traditional law firms look really very vulnerable, especially in a less structured market.

Unless the profession collectively wakes up to the fact that it cannot continue to charge high fees for something that a Google search will reveal for free, it is probably signing a warrant for a slow and painful demise. I am obviously not suggesting that Google is a legal knowledge management system without risk; but it is a system all clients know and all clients use – and it's free.

I may be wrong, after all today is just a moment in time with many options still open to everyone, but for me the direction seems clear – in future knowledge is going to be valued less, so we must ensure wisdom is valued more.

Will clients pay for wisdom? I think they will. A law firm that can genuinely help a client to a successful outcome (or avoid a disastrous one) is adding significant real value. We should all be prepared to pay for that. The challenge is for relationships to be so strong that the relationship itself carries trust and therefore value. In the context of a longer term, mutual gains approach, the law firm should be able to trust the client to give away a great deal; and the client should be commercially savvy enough to pay for wisdom.

Time will tell. For the time being there are therefore two questions unanswered: First can law firms re-engineer their offering to break free of the past, so that they charge a premium for their wisdom while allowing ever cheaper access to knowledge? Second, will clients be brave enough to properly reward wisdom even if the time on the clock is modest? It won't be easy, but I think the alternatives are worse...

FED UP WITH THE
FREE TRAINING FARRAGO...

I may seem a bit ranty on this, but frankly this is a subject long overdue for a good kicking.

Law firms offer free training to clients and contacts. The way this works is that typically clients rock up for a breakfast or an evening session for a croissant or a canapé and an hour or so of presentation on the subject of the moment followed by a bit of limp marketing/networking.

So much is wrong with this (and my apologies for shouting):

It isn't training, it isn't marketing and it isn't free.

For participants, it isn't designed to test you, challenge you, encourage you or motivate you to be different... It is mostly about sitting in a room, half listening (half BlackBerrying) to someone talking to slides, with at least one cheek on the fence, about the latest cases or legislation. In effect it is an audio/visual article/newsletter and while it is hopefully interesting, it probably is not useful and it isn't training you.

Neither is this properly networking. Mostly we hang in a corner hoping there might be one person we recognise who we then cling to through the whole session. The law firm will, on a given signal, send in a few of their new sniffer dog puppies (young partners) to try out their soft selling skills and everyone is frankly relieved when that bit is over and we can all go back to our day jobs...

Finally it isn't free. There is obviously a cost to the law firm for sure. This cost will be met from earnings which in turn will come from their work for their clients...you have already paid for it in advance.

So why does it happen like this?

I think the law firms feel they have to offer this stuff because many clients bang on about it and clients are pre-occupied with harvesting free CPD; but it is a sham dressed up as something it clearly isn't.

The Emperor is naked again. Worst of all it is a colossal waste of time, energy and is a travesty of professional development.

And yet a whole cottage industry exists in many firms to provide this so called added value. A whole industry built around offering sessions to clients a third of whom, typically, are "no-shows"...That is not turning up to events which they have confirmed they want to attend. Is there anything more pathetic than a table full of unclaimed name badges and a poor marketing assistant still trying to do the marketing smile?

We are all guilty of perpetuating this nonsense. We have got it badly wrong and we should therefore do something about it...but what? In my opinion, four things to start:

Law firms – just stop doing this...Partners don't really want to do it and you are pretty average at leveraging marketing value from it...Frankly the content would be easier to appreciate if you popped it on a thoughtful email or put up a short video clip on your website.

In-house teams – just stop asking for it...Don't kid yourselves this is training; don't say you value it, then not turn up and finally why not actually think about the personal and professional development that you do want instead of treating it like a tick-box hygiene factor.

Can we please stop calling it "free" and get some transparency into the cost of law firm engagement. We are buying legal services first and foremost...if we want other things let's discuss that seriously and in detail. Calling it "free" is like buying a Happy Meal for the gift; we are grown-ups now and this is not about the toys.

Can we all please treat personal and professional development as a serious, important and value enhancing process that requires thoughtfulness, energy and planning...

Okay, I shall now dismount the hobby-horse and have a nice calming cup of tea...

AND THE DIFFERENCE IS...

What is the key difference working in-house and in a law firm...?

This is a pretty important question if you are contemplating a move from one to the other; or trying to make sense of the feelings you have now that you have taken that leap...and just as important if you are simply trying to forge a decent working relationship between lawyers in-house and externally.

I won't use this short blog to make the obvious points... but I would like to dive into the psychology of the different roles and why it can undo people in the early stages of their new in-house career.

In a law firm you are valued for making rain (a slightly odd concept for a British lawyer...one seems to have an abundance of damp in one's life, but no doubt the term is meant to denote the importance of rain to the cycle of life - or something!)

Anyway...rain makers make activity; they generate work and build out the opportunity to bill more. In short, the busier you are the more revered you become...Activity, activity, activity is all you have to focus on.

Do the hours, submit the bills, do more hours.

What is more the busier you get the more you can leverage your colleagues. No matter how busy you become it will not matter; there is a seemingly limitless resource to help you; and all the while you are LOVED by your colleagues.

Then you move in-house and you will bounce through the first few weeks like a new puppy and your colleagues will love you too.

Bring me your problems and all your matters, nothing is too much trouble... "I would LOVE to help" is all you have to say...and the work will tumble towards you like an avalanche of email and paper.

...And then you will kill yourself trying to do it

No associates to leverage, no back up resources, not much of a library, few precedents, no budget to go outside, systems that grind to a halt for anything out of the norm...

This is death by a thousand unmet expectations.

You see, in-house you are not valued for creating activity, but for first managing it, then prioritising it and then reducing it. The less work you have to do yourself – by putting in place process, self-help tools, training etc or simply taking a sensible view on risk – the better. As a result you create a structure with more resilience, less dependency and more aligned to the profit and loss of your business.

Importantly this will then free you to focus on the things that properly matter and not to silt-up under the burden of low risk, repetitive, and unending "rats and mice" work...

You will still be busy – heaven knows you will be busy – but unless you can reduce demand for your personal time, then prioritise and manage what is left, you are sunk.

So if you move in-house you must forget all you ever knew about being a rain maker...you are now flood defences and chief mopper-upper.

THE HIDDEN BURDEN
OF THE GENERAL COUNSEL ROLE

In another life I once held positions as General Counsel in two major companies and so watching the News International phone hacking story play out in the press and on television I cannot help having a thought for Tom Crone and wondering what he must be going through now and what it was like for him when he was at N.I.

I am not going to write about Mr Crone now; it would not be fair and I have no view on the rights or wrongs of the situations he might have faced; but it does raise a concern that I have had for some time and one that I would like to write about.

Approximately every couple of weeks or so I get a call from a General Counsel who would like to chat something through; the call will start with a few superficial comments about how we might have met once before a couple of year ago, or how the call was prompted by an article (or something) ...but then we will get to the point of the call and it is rarely a comfortable listen.

Over the last five or six years I have heard most things...

My chief executive bullies me;

The marketing director doesn't follow advice;

I am certain we are breaking the law in x or y manner;

We are not reporting on something the regulator wants to see.

...And very many more examples like these.

I do not want to pretend that in-house lawyers are grappling with illegality or unethical practices as part of the every-day routine; but I am certain that many General Counsel occasionally feel exposed and in need of some support.

One of the first such calls I had was about seven years ago and concerned a company that had gone into administration. The sole in-house lawyer had been working on a property matter which had failed to complete when his business literally ran out of cash. The law firm acting for the landlord had sent him a Friday pm email which just said:

"Your email of last week confirmed your company would be in funds and ready to complete. This amounts to an undertaking for which you are personally and professionally responsible."

The poor guy told me this while crying his eyes out.

In the end the Landlord did not pursue the undertaking and the lawyer involved "only" lost his job and nothing else. It was however my first real-life encounter with the hidden burden of the General Counsel role.

I am very fortunate to work with some really able in-house lawyers who brilliantly manage not just the legal risk of their businesses, but who have genuinely established themselves as respected trusted advisors to their employers. However I also know that many very able in-house lawyers find themselves locked into structures that do not easily facilitate access to the CEO or board, where their remit is limited to operational priorities and where many decisions are taken without a thought of running it past them...

Another call I took last year was from a General Counsel based in Europe whose business was under investigation for fraud. A senior employee told him not to worry so much as there would be an "elegant solution" involving unauthorised payments. The General Counsel subsequently resigned.

I have long held the view that companies taking on the privilege of employing qualified lawyers should fully appreciate the extent of their lawyers' professional duties AND that in-house lawyers should fully embrace their role as officers of the court and as exemplars of a strict ethical code.

We talk long and hard about lawyers partnering with business, of being commercially focussed facilitators and of being proactive, but we must do this in a context which will sometimes mean difficult conversations and sometimes very difficult decisions. In the end relationship management is not about pleasing people, but about doing the right things.

My view is that business should welcome this from the board level down, but we must also help businesses and lawyers make this work well. To be a General Counsel is potentially one of the most intellectually rewarding and important positions to achieve in any company. It may also be a profoundly lonely and isolating role.

I will leave you with three thoughts:

First, every General Counsel should have someone they respect and trust and who they can talk to when the going gets particularly tough. Experienced General Counsel out there, please put yourself forward for mentoring roles and relationship partners in law firms – I am talking to you here too – step up to the plate please

Second, General Counsel – when was the last time you read the SRA guidance on code of conduct? You must know this stuff and how to build internal and external support structures around you.

Finally, just take care; it can be tough out there.

SPECIALISATION –
BENEFIT OR BURDEN?

...Almost from the moment a lawyer hatches from the chrysalis of their training contract they will specialise. A butterfly is born, but one that feeds on a very narrow diet. I have often wondered if this is a burden or a benefit...

I suppose on the one hand it means that the "Big Law" law firms can claim to bring specialist depth in a variety of subject disciplines, presumably charge premium fees for their expertise and rock-up to meetings with a small tribe of eager fee earners. And, if I am generous, the advantage to the client is that they may be able to buy deep insight that potentially affords competitive advantage...

But there are downsides too...labelled and routed (as well as rooted) lawyers are pushed towards knowing more and more about an area that will have less and less relevance to an ever increasing number of potential contacts and clients.

This isn't "strategic"; it is instead a gamble on matching a market with a career...More concerning still is that I do not believe for a moment this is what the vast majority of corporate clients actually want.

Most clients care less that their lawyer is steeped in specialty, dripping with technical insight; but they do care about good judgement and wisdom and that their lawyer has the character and personality to encourage them to invest their faith and trust in the outcomes of their lawyer's work. If this sounds a bit "airy-fairy", let me put it this way: Clients want lawyers who make good decisions based on the right amount of information. A decision with no facts is a guess. A decision with all facts will be too late. Judgement is deciding how many facts are needed. Wisdom is getting it right.

I am not suggesting that when some esoteric tax point is in issue or when a "bet the company" takeover is being planned that the true rocket scientists of the profession are not needed or value for money – whatever they cost. I am certain however that for maybe 75% of the legal work that is done on behalf of corporate clients, specialism is more hindrance than help. It results in tactical advice not strategic advice; it creates duplication and slows things down. It is designed to improve time sheets, not to get to a desired outcome in a commercial and timely way.

Some of the best lawyers I know would proclaim that they know precious little law. Working with, for example, top General Counsel, one can see how they have moved through specialism to a more important place. They understand risk, understand (more importantly) their business's tolerance to risk; they apply their analytical skills, relationship development skills, their creative problem solving skills, their influencing skills and their communication skills...In doing so they are seen as a contributor, a player, a voice at the table that should be heard.

All lawyers should aspire for their guidance to be perceived in this way and all lawyers should see that the majority of their corporate clients want an experience like this too. This isn't rocket science, but it is very clever.

Please do not misunderstand me. This is not a charter for the slap-dash and the partially ignorant. I am certain of course that lawyers must be trained to know and apply the law; and I do not belittle the importance of rigour and discipline in this pursuit. I am really making a plea for balance.

It is the case, for example, that with genuinely excellent on-line resources, with automation and the ever increasing sophistication of systems and processes, pure legal expertise has become more accessible and for a much lower cost than ever before. This appears to be a trend that will only continue. In effect it results in a levelling of the playing field so that across a range of lawyers and law firms one cannot easily distinguish between them on legal expertise alone.

If therefore we cannot easily choose between one lawyer and another based on their legal know-how, clients are bound to make distinctions/choices based on other criteria. The sort of criteria I mention above when referring to the General Counsel skills set. Increasingly therefore we can also anticipate that knowing the law will be seen as little more than "hygiene" factor, while the application of know-how will be the value add.

Put simply the positive perception of value by clients is less and less influenced by what lawyers know and more and more influenced by how lawyers use know-how to make a difference to the clients they serve.

Perhaps even more importantly clients are realising that legal advice should not just provide a useable solution (lovely though that would be!), but that it should be capable of resulting in competitive advantage. This can only happen however when there is a deep understanding of the client's interests in a business, risk and socio-economic context. In effect legal advice is becoming a strategic indicator of value.

For me this is the difference between information and wisdom. Information will continue to be reduced in price to the point when it may even be given away free; wisdom however will carry a high margin and rightly so.

The sooner we therefore start to systematically, thoughtfully and determinedly train our lawyers in business skills, soft skills and in developing leadership credentials, the better it will be for them and for their clients.

THE "WHAT", THE "SO WHAT" AND THE "NOW WHAT"

One of my colleagues uses a line regularly when we are assessing how to turn a nice warm, fluffy idea into something that has some colder edges and a little more recognisable reality about it...

He will say: "We know what the 'what' is...But does it pass the 'so what' test and, if it does, 'now what'?

It goes to the heart something we feel quite strongly about:

- ...We don't like initiative fatigue, where the focus on strategising defeats delivery
- We don't like it at all when we are asked if we can knock-up some KPI's, as if performance is less important and can be separated from the ideas that are meant to drive excellence
- We are not terribly enamoured of the scrabble for objectives (SMART, LEAN, Six Sigma'd or otherwise) which are not co-ordinated nor present continuity of performance in the annual round of how to justify a bonus.

In my view it isn't being "strategic" if all you end up doing is shoe-horning a half-baked idea into some HR inspired balanced scorecard template thingy.

And neither is it being "strategic" if you use valuable time and energy concocting self-serving, woolly and clichéd-riddled platitudes and then pass them off as cutting edge thinking.

So, let's cut to the point...ideas are easy, cheap and cheerful...There can be real energy in a room when ideas are bouncing around and it can be a lot of fun too...rethinking anything is usually worthwhile.

The challenge however is usually not "can you think of an idea?" The challenge is properly a) can you evaluate the worth of the idea and b) do you know how to implement it if it is worth doing?

This brings me to something that is troubling me a lot about the profession's response to the Legal Services Act...

I am not one of those people who thinks that this is the death knell for all that was once successful, noble and ethical about lawyers; nor do I think that everything newly announced or just launched will be wonderful or even a suitable response to some intractable problems.

All that glisters is not necessarily Quality.

What frustrates is that for the most part I am just bored by the sterility of the debate which hasn't even begun to analyse whether the new services and propositions that are out there are worth anything (to their owners, employees and customers) and whether they have a chance of succeeding.

It's like we are fixated with whether the brand name works or not; or whether sticking a logo on a poster at a railway station is classy or not.

It is possibly entertaining to write/present a polemic about the end of something on the one hand, or a new dawn on the other; but frankly this is just so much blah, blah...

It might be interesting, but it ain't useful...and we need to move on from being the legal equivalent of Nostradamuses (Nostradamii?)

The people I am interested in (and admire) are those who are getting on and implementing their plans... Of course some will undoubtedly fail, but many won't... and some will be genuine game changers.

These are people (only some of them lawyers note) who are addressing the 'so what?' and 'now what?' questions...

They are really clever.

They have not just had an "away day" to discuss the "value" they might bring and rehashed a mission statement; instead they have modelled the service, understood their costs, developed their materials, assessed the opportunity for scaling their concepts and calculated its return on investment etc, etc.

They have build process, created infrastructure, persuaded investors to join them and convinced themselves that it is a challenge and a risk worth pursuing. This is to be admired.

It might also be why the legal profession (which is seemingly still debating whether to even look into what ABS might mean) is heading for some darker days if it doesn't wake up.

We need to care a lot less about whether to be up-in-arms about how jolly slip-shod it has all become (not like it was in my day, etc) and a darn sight more engaged with how markets are being assessed (even created), what the margins might be, how scalable it all is and whether we have the skills to exploit the opportunities.

So whether you are the managing partner in a law firm contemplating merger, investment, joint venture etc...

Or a General Counsel looking at resource deployment, what value means to your colleagues and how risk management can deliver competitive advantage...

...Make sure you move quickly from the 'what' to the 'so what' to the 'then what'.

WHAT MAKES A GREAT LAWYER?

...The essence of becoming a great lawyer is realising that it isn't about you.

This is hard...after all, after the law degree, law school, training, qualifying, trying to make your way, putting up with partners behaving like four-year-olds and working your socks off...of course it should be about you!

...But it isn't.

It's not really even about what you know. Obviously you have to know a great deal about the law; your technical skill set is precious and important and is your ticket to play; but it doesn't make you a great lawyer.

It's not about who you work for either...having a successful letterhead to write on is an advantage, might open doors, might do some of the early hard yards in helping you build your personal credentials – but at the end of the day it is just a letterhead and does not make you a great lawyer.

So what does?

Being a great lawyer is about three things:

1. Accepting unequivocally that it is not about you
2. Recognising that for all the law you know and the brilliance of your mind, what you know is just a ticket to ride, and finally and crucially...
3. To be able to work inside the client's head

And it is this third element that I would like to focus on; it is the key to everything.

Clients come in all shapes and sizes – huge multi-national telecos, government backed institutions, the banks, fleet-of-foot technology companies etc; and the first mistake a lawyer makes is to think they act for these companies –

they do not. They act for individuals within the companies.

Professionally, of course, the lawyer acts in the best interests of the company, but in reality the challenge is not working with an "entity", but to work with real people within the entity who have personal targets, hopes, ambitions, fears...People, as well, who have different levels of understanding, different tolerances to risk and who, frankly, have good days and bad days.

The most important skill for any lawyer with aspirations to be a great lawyer therefore is the ability to listen.

It sounds too easy, but therein probably lays the trap. It sounds easy, but it is VERY hard to do well.

I hope that being charming, calm, professional and reassuring are positive characteristics of most lawyers (although we will all know many for whom this is a significant stretch!) but how many of us properly listen?

Listening is not just about taking an accurate note of instruction, it is also about understanding what lies behind the words; what is the ambition of the people involved for the matter in question; where are their vulnerabilities, their blind spots, their assumptions, their misplaced faith, their likely challenges.

In so doing the lawyer can not only discern a preferred course, but also the most acceptable tone of voice; to have alternative courses of action in mind when things hit problems and to have the language and the demeanour that reassures, challenges and inspires when that is necessary too.

Listening is fundamental to your success and yet it will not appear on any law school syllabus and it is rarely systematically coached once you begin your legal career. Instead we elevate a few who intuitively "get it" and call them rain-makers and for the rest of us we are assigned the task of getting busy so we can worship at the altar of activity and the hourly rate!

This is so wrong...All clients (that is people in clients) want to feel that their lawyers understand their interests, priorities, concerns and hopes. It really does not take much to engage around these issues; to explore, encourage, facilitate and develop ideas through conversation, by listening and validating your interpretation... And all of us are capable of doing this so much better than we typically do today.

Once lawyers have invested in their glass towers, have created their brand strategies and their sector expertise, they will look around and still be faced with the same clients with the same human concerns – very few of which are addressed by having a lift that goes to the thirtieth floor or a glossy brochure that is created by a reassuringly expensive creative consultant.

The towers, the brochures, the art etc are not statements about client listening, they are statements that say "look at us – aren't we successful" and "look at us – we must know a lot and be very clever"!

...In a way, all fine. It is a competitive place and lawyers need to compete with each other as much as for clients – but whatever you do, never confuse this for what your clients want.

Being a great lawyer does not depend on the view from your office window but whether you can visualise what your client sees when they ask you for your help.

I PREDICT A RIOT...

For a few nights in August 2011 some streets in London, Manchester and Birmingham were temporarily taken over by, predominantly, young people who systematically and violently smashed, grabbed, looted and burned their way through the night. They acted, it seems, without fear, without a thought to the consequences of their behaviour and with reckless disregard for their safety and the safety of others. It was an extraordinary sight and one that will stay a long time in the memory of those who witnessed it on television. For those who live in the affected communities they may never fully come to terms with what happened and it will take months, perhaps years for communities to recover from the physical scars.

Now in the immediate aftermath we see the media typically try to simplify and thereby polarise the debate – on the one hand the liberal left blaming a lack of social cohesion, relative poverty and a lack of meaningful life opportunities, and on the conservative right a desire to treat the acts as purely those of criminal thuggery and deserving only of the strongest criminal justice punishments available.

The sound-bite media culture we live in forces the polarisation of the debate and while it might make good television it is not insightful in any meaningful way.

So, hesitatingly, I would like to offer a non-polarising viewpoint and to join in the debate. Before doing so I should say that I am not an expert in any relevant field and neither do I have the perspective of some relevant real life experience to draw upon. Indeed I only have the perspective of a middle-aged, professional white male. I presume I have very little in common with the urban poor teenager; although my family was certainly not wealthy. However, I did not consider myself poor and in many ways I had an idyllic childhood with a loving family in a rural small town. Expectations were more modest and I had no notion of being disenfranchised. If I am honest I had no notion of being enfranchised either.

My views therefore are not important to the media or to the so called "chattering classes" but I hope that does not mean I have no voice. So, with your indulgence I will take a few minutes of your day if you continue to read on...

For centuries the poor have rioted. They have rioted over the lack of food, property and political influence. They have rioted against the established orthodoxy and between themselves. It is not new and the only people who ever seem surprised are those who have plenty of food, wealth and political influence.

I believe however, that we all have it within us to be angered by unfairness and injustice whether over the closure of a school, hospital or factory; or, more significantly, when our families and communities are at risk of physical harm. Indeed in extremis we all have it within us to be destructive in a cause as well.

The mindset appears to be that in order to have a voice one must first be heard, and if we are not heard we will seek alternative and sometimes destructive, even self-destructive, means in order to be heard.

So, for example, workers will strike for better pay and conditions; but strikes cost those participating in them real money and may even cost them their jobs. These people will therefore destroy and harm their own wellbeing if the cause is worth it.

In times of war, predominantly young people can be mobilised to defend their way of life and their communities;

but many will be killed and injured in doing so. In times of political revolution, predominantly young people will put themselves in harm's way and may even participate in destroying the physical infrastructure they seek to protect and preserve.

I am sure there are very many more examples of affirmative action risking physical harm to people and property when we collectively feel mobilised to act. Before I am labelled an apologist for criminal behaviour, I should point out that I am not blind to the fact that within these constructs, bad people do bad things. The mistreatment of prisoners of war, the rape and assault of innocent civilians by occupying powers, the political and social corruption that follows dismantled commercial norms, the looting of property by opportunists and the settling of scores by rival gangs...these are all examples of criminal behaviour, sometimes on an industrial scale, that can flourish in the civil vacuum that is created by disruptive behaviour.

How we view the balance between criminal disruption and legitimate grievance in part depends on our proximity to the acts, our personal empathy with those involved and the distance we have in time to judge the actions in a broader context.

The young men and women who took to the streets in August in London, Manchester and Birmingham will have had many motivations and some of those motivations will have changed over the course of the days they were involved. Many will have felt angry and aggrieved some without necessarily knowing precisely what about or why...anger is not always a well directed emotion after all.

Some of them as well will have just seen an opportunity for a fight; while some others will have been caught up in the adrenalin rush of something crazy happening in the streets they live in.

I don't think we can judge today with clarity or certainty why it happened and what lessons there are to draw from what happened. All I think we can say is that for a thousand years and more some people who have perceived themselves to be dispossessed, disconnected and disenfranchised have fought back when they felt that hopelessness was all they owned.

Then, depending on the kindliness (or not) of the historian's perspective, we review such riotous acts of the poor as either the legitimate and honourable fight for rights and freedoms, or the misguided nastiness and folly of a criminally motivated minority.

I hope politicians have the sense and wisdom to pause before they act, but I predict they will not. I hope that we can build communities where we do not disengage and disenfranchise a significant minority of young people, but I predict we will always do so. I hope we may not have riots in future because we have addressed the legitimate concerns of the urban poor, but I fear we will not and sadly therefore, I predict a riot.

TO INFLUENCE...
IS THIS THE GREATEST SKILL OF ALL?

If you were to ask lawyers what their ultimate client compliment would be then many will say that it is to be considered a "trusted advisor". It doesn't matter if these lawyers work in-house or in law firms the phrase "trusted advisor" seems to have a very special resonance which goes to the essence of what being a lawyer means to them.

I have thought about this phrase a great deal, examined examples where it has been achieved (and not) and analysed what it might actually mean in practice. In this article I will explore the steps lawyers can take that will help them move along the relationship development pathway towards becoming a "trusted advisor" to their clients.

The headline conclusion of what this phrase means will not be surprise; the essence of being a trusted advisor is to be influential.

One of the most rewarding days of my career as a lawyer was when my then Chief Executive, with whom I did not always have the warmest of relationships, said to our Sales Director "I agree, but subject to what Paul says"... In that moment I knew that my judgement was trusted and that I was regarded as someone with influence whose judgement was considered neither partial nor self-motivated and whose views would be offered in the best interests of the company.

This was not about the quality of my legal expertise (how would they know if my technical knowledge of legal regulation was accurate or not?), but about the quality of relationships I had developed and the sense those colleagues had of my judgement and of me as a person.

This point in my career however was not achieved quickly – It took a number of years for me to reach this level of acceptance; so what is this concept that we have called "influence"? Can it be trained or coached? And how do we know how well we are doing? I think there are five stages to becoming more influential and therefore to becoming a trusted advisor:

1. Have a track record of decision making that demonstrates more often than not that you make good calls. No one is ever 100% right 100% of the time, but do you make decisions that generally have good outcomes? There are two related and crucial points to make – first be seen to make decisions and second make sure the outcomes from your good decisions are seen as well!

2. Develop a work ethic that puts colleagues' interests and concerns before your own. There is no need to be continuously burning the midnight oil (although some will be involved inevitably) but be seen to work hard in a committed, non partisan and not self-serving way.

3. Show a willingness and a curiosity to be engaged across your colleagues/clients business and be genuinely interested in their people, products and services. Be passionate for their worlds and they will invest more in yours.

4. Demonstrate a generosity of spirit that praises publically the good work of others, but which also offers a quiet private word when things could and should have been done better.

5. Have an appetite for being involved in the non legal projects and initiatives that are the personal concern of senior managers. To be influential you will need to reach out from behind your desk and become involved in work that is not just about the law.

Earlier, I posed the question can this be trained or coached? The answer is undoubtedly that it can, but if you find yourself attending a half day workshop entitled "Influencing skills for lawyers" it will most probably be too superficial to be useful and may seem a little trite. I believe developing influencing skills requires a deeper and more thoughtful approach. It is an approach I can summarise in six short points:

1. Be good at presentation across all media – a thoughtful email, a well chosen comment and insightful recommendation etc, will carry impact. The more presentation skills are practiced, developed and honed the better.

2. Be visible – listen a lot, contribute thoughtfully, but not too much and ensure you have an opinion. Having an opinion does not mean forcing your view; it just means engaging in the debate. You must be seen to be part of the environment and culture, not separate from it – If colleagues can say about you "I don't really know what he/she thinks" it will be so much harder for you to become influential and therefore a trusted advisor.

3. Have good project skills – ensure you have initiatives of your own and be seen to deliver successfully against your targets and objectives.

4. Be a generous networker – be prepared to share your ideas, help others in their concerns. The more you share, the more will be shared with you.

5. Set the highest ethical and professional standards for your own conduct and that of your team. Do not wear "professionalism" on your sleeve, but ensure commitments are kept (always) and never, ever, give anyone the slightest cause for concern about your motivation

6. Be patient – the tipping point will not always be obvious and may be at different points for different colleagues. The challenge is not to force people to respect your work, but to ensure that what they see of you and the way you work will resonate with them.

Present well, be visible, project manage, network, be ethical and patient – all these points are about building influence over time in a disciplined, systematic and thoughtful way. It is just one among many important skills, but in my opinion it is THE core skill for all successful lawyers. It is the window through which others will judge your talent, your commitment and your judgement – and it doesn't get any more significant than that...

GO FETCH A SENSE OF PURPOSE

I was taking a walk in one of London's many beautiful squares; It was through Lincoln's Inn at 730am a week or so ago. A thin mist was clinging to the grass, not a cloud in the sky and with the early morning sunshine lighting the scene, but not yet warming the air.

As I turned a corner in the square a small dog ran past me at full tilt in hot pursuit of a stick thrown by his master. The dog was mighty pleased with himself and trotted back past me in the opposite direction, bouncing on his paws, stick clenched between his teeth.

As I walked on I reflected a little on what I had just seen. Obviously I had seen a man throw a stick that his dog then ran after to collect....but what I had actually seen was something more important. You see it's not about the stick and it's not about the dog – it's about being the dog that is asked to fetch the stick.

We all need a purpose to feel fulfilled; the absence of purpose leaves us feeling a little lost, a little vulnerable and potentially undone...a dog without a stick to chase.

And what you may ask is the purpose of this little meander? It is that lawyers need a purpose too; but not the purpose of just making money – as important as that is; or of behaving ethically (ditto). I think lawyers work best when they feel an empathy with their client, a commitment beyond the instruction and a sense of belonging with the client as part of the client's team. In other words lawyers should be trying to create a purpose for their work that goes beyond the activity.

I do not think this is a surprising view, I do find it surprising however how few lawyers embrace this idea as wholeheartedly as they should.

Asserting purpose and commitment is not enough. If this is to happen then actions and changes to behaviour are needed too. In the next few sentences I share some ideas that I think can help lawyers deliver their service with purpose and in doing so be more fulfilled.

Ten ideas:

1. Understanding the client's true interests to align the service not just to the issues, but to the client's tolerance to risk, their sense of what is an acceptable outcome, the broader context (commercial, reputational etc) and in a proportionate and cost effective way.
2. Always to see issues in the context of future risk management and/or competitive advantage. In other words, learning the lessons from all activity so that processes are improved, risks mitigated and opportunities exploited.
3. Never missing an opportunity to inform, educate and train the client to show how their actions can avoid subsequent lawyer intervention or at least keep it to a minimum.
4. Exploiting your networks to the commercial advantage of the client and leveraging know-how without having to be asked.
5. Being articulate and passionate about the client's products and services, using the vocabulary of the client, understanding their ambitions, plans and objectives. Never ever giving the impression that for the lawyer this is "just another gig".
6. Looking out for the people in the client teams so that you are aware of key moments for them too (promotions,

new projects, recruitment drives, cost cutting initiatives etc). Not to do this in a quasi manipulative way, but just to take a normal human interest.

7. Always being able to articulate value. Most lawyers can say what something costs (after the event at least), but are less adept at translating that number into either a comparator – "so we saved £xyz relative to abc"; or at making a real terms cost reduction or profit improvement. There is no need for lawyers to become accountants, but lawyers must be able to translate their activity into a business literate vocabulary.

8. Being proactive – not for its own sake, but with the purpose of seeking to be constructively influential with key people at important moments; in effect to be strategic in a proportionate and not self-serving way. Seek access to influence, but once there do not dwell. It is about seizing an opportune moment to make a difference, not a right to occupy.

9. Challenge the client to be better too. Let us all be the best we can be and relish the opportunity for improvement in effectiveness and efficiency. Then be determined to deliver; you want to be a player so act like one; gentlemanly indifference or studied patience will not endear you to a client that might need you to take the initiative sometimes.

10. Celebrate with the client when things go well and commiserate with the client when they don't. To share the joy of success and the burden of failure is to be part of the team, not a spectator of it.

Going back to where I began and my walk in Lincoln's Inn, the dog who was asked to fetch the stick had a genuine purpose. The ten ideas outlined here are designed to create a similar sense of belonging and to recognise the power derived from a strong relationship.

In the end it will not be the technical quality of your work that will enable you to create a sense of purpose. It will be whether you have done enough beyond the legal work for the client to want to invest in building the relationship with you.

O.M.G ...I HAVE STARTED TO TWEET

A larming though the headline may be I do not mean that I have started to make the sound made by small birds; I mean I am now participating in the social-media phenomenon that is "Twitter".

If this does not distress you too much dear reader and you can be bothered then please by all means look me up at @LBCWiseCounsel.

So what is a middle-aged man of (usually) sound mind doing messing about on the micro-blogging website made famous by D-list celebrities telling the world what they ate for breakfast?

I must admit that I was a sceptic. I could not see what possible value there might be in something so seemingly trivial. I could not have been more wrong and I wish I had not waited so long. I can honestly say that it has been a genuinely enriching experience and for lots of different reasons.

- Saying something useful in 140 characters (including spaces) is difficult and a great discipline to practice. A good friend and client of mine who is the global General Counsel of a major telecoms brand told me recently that he now tries to write all his email messages to executive colleagues so that they can be read in the space provided by a single BlackBerry screen. The world is a complex place and of course brevity is not always good, but most messages would benefit from editing. Could Twitter be the start of a revolution in lawyers being less verbose?!

- The diversity of opinion on Twitter is fascinating. I'm not going to pretend that everyone is readable or even intelligible - it is of course easy to find people who want to tell you to love the world or that their morning muffin tasted nice; but it is equally easy to find in-depth opinion, insightful comment, challenge and intellect. In the UK, for example the thoughts of contributors such as @LegalBrat, @Kilroyt, @BugsieGiven, @CharonQC and @LegalBizzle may sound a little unpromising just from their names, but in just a few weeks I have come to realise that these folks (all with big and serious legal roles) and very many others are sharing information, opinion and insight that is relevant, useful, clever and kind. It is a resource like no other I have ever seen before.

- What is especially impressive however is how dialogue develops so that information and opinions are not just posted, but debated. In real time Tweeters can watch and/or contribute and in doing so thoughts are challenged and developed in a way that is just not possible with print. For example, if you disagree with this last thought I may never know; but if I make the same point on Twitter, and you disagreed with me, I would know instantly. That's not just clever, it is enriching as well.

- I will be fifty on my next birthday – I have two teenage daughters and to be honest I am not sure I have ever properly understood the fascination of BEBO, Facebook or MySpace – it has been (largely continues to be) a mystery to me. However the power of social networking in the way that they practice it is now something that is much more real to me. To be able to simultaneously connect across the country, across the world with multiple contributors and on myriad subjects/themes is mind-boggling, but it is also joyful. The world is a smaller, more accessible place and better for sharing opinion.

- Within in a few clicks I can now regularly exchange views with law students, trainees, academics, journalists, partners in law firms and in-house lawyers; I can do it instantly and from any location. I can test my views, challenge others and listen to many opinions I would never otherwise access, while at all times I can also simply observe human interaction on some really important issues.

- Even in the last few weeks I have also seen more law firms enter the space – partners and associates dipping their toes in the social network waters and for the most part enjoying the relaxed, informal, but insightful banter. It may be my slightly jaundiced view, but I think Twitter may prove to be an antidote to the overly processed and homogenised slick marketing machines of the major law firms. Instead we can see real people with real opinions and I believe they will benefit from that exposure significantly.

- What I have also appreciated however is the generosity of spirit – Tweeters sharing links to published articles, to online resources and to other contributors who might help. It is a medium, so far, mercifully free of corporate messages and contributors angling for commercial advantage. It is charmingly, old fashioned and benign networking in its truest sense; and represents the precedence of community interests over self interests.

I would certainly encourage you to be involved – if nothing else it will challenge you to write more succinctly than you ever thought possible! Imagine saying anything in 140 characters (including spaces) that is useful and interesting and you'll see what I mean.

So will Twitter change the world? There are commentators

who think it already has in terms of the mobilisation of people to protest. At one level therefore it is already "game-changing" – however more gently there is an impact at a more individual level, because while in the grand scheme of things I am quite sure that I will not change the world by anything I Tweet, my world has already been changed for the better by those whose Tweets I follow.

THE BIGGEST TEST OF ALL

I am not one for polemic exaggeration or self-serving controversy, so please believe me when I say I would like to write about what I consider to be the biggest test of all for lawyers.

It is not an exaggeration, but a genuine and passionate concern. And the test I want to describe is not just the biggest test this year, or even this decade, but the biggest test in the last one hundred years, perhaps the biggest test since the time when being a lawyer was first recognised as the second oldest profession on planet earth.

The question in my mind is this: "What is a lawyer?" ...and the test is: "What is the point of being a lawyer?"

Okay, let's move on from the obvious...we all know that a lawyer is someone who has studied law, taken professional exams and is authorised by a body (Law Society) confirming that a minimum standard of attainment has been achieved; I get that, but the question remains – what actually is a lawyer? What does a lawyer do that someone who is not a lawyer cannot do?

A few years ago it was easier to answer; lawyers had a regulatory monopoly to do certain types of work (in the UK for example – probate, conveyancing and High Court litigation). Lawyers also had to work in law firms or be employed in in-house roles.

Over time however these limits have been relaxed. Property work can be undertaken by licensed conveyancers and much more importantly the Legal Services Act will shortly permit entities other than traditional law firms to undertake legal work. We already have Legal Process

Outsourcers in India, South Africa and elsewhere; and we have commoditised legal "factories" processing thousands of routine personal injury cases with minimal human supervision.

Furthermore even today, as long as I do not hold myself out to be a lawyer, I could set up a business to advise clients on employment matters, on contract management and dispute resolution.

Where will we be if all these developments continue at a similar rate in say five years from now?

There are other significant trends to note as well. In my early career as a lawyer I was an in-house solicitor and I was fortunate to become a General Counsel in two major financial services companies. I was definitely and proudly a lawyer, but even then – over ten years ago – I was conscious of something that increasingly played on my mind. What was I doing that had to be done by a lawyer? I did not do property work or litigation (I was a regulatory lawyer); I did not give legal advice although I managed a team of lawyers, I contributed to debates with executive colleagues, I managed some big projects and I helped my businesses to be aware of and manage legal risk.

...And precisely none of this required me to be qualified.

Then there is the very real point about really good real lawyers, which is that all the time they are advising their clients they happily blur the line between what is legal advice and what is commercial acumen. So where does the legal advice end and the commercial savvy begin?

In the decade since I stopped being a proper lawyer the in-house legal sector has grown in influence and standing, but nearly all in-house lawyers do not need a practice certificate and could operate in their businesses competently, professionally and appreciated, but essentially unregulated.

Now with the further relaxation of the professional monopoly and the advent of new "Alternative Business Structures" the legal profession faces a very VERY significant identity crisis. What does being a lawyer bring to the party that justifies the qualification?

Add into the mix the rise of the legal publishers making access to legal know-how more affordable and more understandable than ever before. Then reflect on the inexorable development of mobile technology, of sophisticated algorithms and smart "apps" that potentially dispense with the need to consult a lawyer in the guise of a human being!

What we might be left with is something deeply shocking, or deeply liberating depending on your point of view. Just what is the point of lawyers for the vast majority of contract, commercial, social welfare, dispute resolution and property activity?

I do not believe the answer will not be revealed in a "Big Bang" moment; the legal profession will not implode, because what I describe are not events, but trends – a sort of long-shore drift slowly reshaping and redistributing power and influence.

What is clear however is that being a lawyer is not a guarantee of working with any degree of exclusivity. Being a lawyer will not mean competing for work just with other lawyers; and being a lawyer, of itself, may not be a competitive advantage or a guarantee of quality.

Lawyers must fundamentally shift their perspective so that investment in technology, know-how and their people is deep, sustained and real – not just by the standards of other law firms, but by the standards of exemplar employers in all sectors and industries. Lawyers must also come to see the supermarkets, banks, publishers (and others) not as potential clients, but as potential competitors.

The incredible conclusion when this comes to pass is that within a relatively short period of time, and certainly before the end of the current decade, if lawyers do not adapt to the new reality, there will be little point in being a lawyer or working in a traditional law firm.

Now you will see why I consider this time to be the biggest test of all.

THE FUTURE TODAY

It is clear that we are working through an extraordinary time for the legal profession; there are so many factors in play that it can feel almost impossible to discern trends. There are however three significant factors that at least provide some context for this period of unprecedented change:

- First, the potential for significant deregulation of legal services heralded by the Legal Services Act which is forcing, at the very least, a dialogue about change
- Second, the consequences of a deep economic recession on client perceptions of cost and value and
- Third the inexorable march of technological innovation.

Many commentators have described this as a "perfect storm" for lawyers and the legal profession. The phrase "perfect storm", in my judgement, however is completely wrong. It is resonant of uncontrollable forces resulting in an inevitable and disastrous conclusion for those unlucky enough to be caught up in it; a misfortune likely to be preceded only by one's passive acceptance that one's lot is up.

While I have long held to the view that change of a significant and sustained nature was bound to impact on the legal profession I have also stated many times that this was the opportunity of a generation to shape a profession for the better. This is clearly a vulnerable time; but is also a time full of positive possibilities.

For lawyers proud of the traditions and history of the great men and women who have shaped the profession before, it is a time to protect and entrench age old ethical values that are too precious to discard; but at the same time to take the really significant strategic and operational strides forward that would have been unimaginable even ten years ago.

Change today is significant and there for all to see. For example many commentators have written about the significance of outsourcing, legal process outsourcing and off-shoring. Even more have bandied around the misnamed "Tesco Law" to speculate on the commoditisation of legal services in a consumer driven revolution that will see retail disciplines applied to professional services.

These are concepts that are real today and potentially significant for years to come; however what I want to write about are the less headline-grabbing, but nevertheless discernible trends that also suggest different models of organisation and delivery. These changes are more subtle, more interesting and will potentially make an even bigger impact.

The problem with "Tesco Law" is that it has become a cliché; there is no longer any analysis, instead it is the unquestioned apotheosis of a deregulated market. In reality I suspect that while the productisation of legal services will continue at a pace; the supermarkets will not be suppliers of legal services, they will be the retailers of personal legal services.

It is entirely reasonable therefore to view such a development as one where lawyers and law firms will benefit. In effect it provides another channel of delivery for their talent and know-how, not a denial of their living.

Off-shoring and legal process outsourcing are more interesting. Law firms (and perhaps some of the biggest corporate and public sector in-house teams) will increasingly view this as an opportunity to take cost out of their processes. This is a little like car assembly plants where the components are manufactured in cheaper lands far away, but assembled and badged in Sunderland or Swindon (or in the case of legal services closer to the Square Mile or Wall Street). For legal services it offers the potential for quality to be reassured through the brand of the supplier, but for the supplier to manage their cost base more effectively and certainly. In a significant way therefore outsourcing and off-shoring is about profit preservation and less about innovation.

What then are the changes that might make an even bigger impact? I think there are four very different and quite subtle shifts in temperament and style that have the potential to be truly revolutionary. I also think that these ideas, while they are not widely seen today, are the very essence of entrepreneurialism; in ten years time I believe we will look back and see their true worth as pointing the way to a completely different approach to legal services. The four ideas can be summed up in this way:

1. Knowledge is power:

Centuries ago the printing of books began a revolution in the dissemination of information that empowered the education of the working classes and accelerated innovation in commerce, the arts and in the sciences. The internet revolution of the last decade is our equivalent today and is doing the same, but in an exponential way. Legal services are being caught up in this revolution too.

Access to justice, in terms of court representation, may still depend for now on the interpretive skills of advocates, but this is only a small part of the access issue. The major players in legal content publishing, companies such as Lexis Nexis and Practical Law Company, have established extraordinarily powerful bases. I am not a great technophile, but the pace of development in mobile technology, in searchable databases, in "intelligent" algorithms brings legal expertise to a far broader audience than ever before.

This is the democratisation of legal services and will drive cost down, in most cases, to a negligible level. Where once a lawyer could charge their time to assess, research and advise, in future a few clicks will give most people most of what they want. I am not judgemental about this and there is clearly risk (for lawyers and consumers) for all to see, but where good is good enough no one can deny the incredible opportunity that the publishers have to bring about unprecedented access to legal expertise that will change commerce, dispute resolution, protection of rights etc forever.

2. Price reduction for richer for poorer

In this world where we pay less and less for the gift of knowledge, will we pay more and more for the wrapping?

I have lectured for years now on this theme; on the one hand even the most discerning purchasers of legal services struggle to articulate how they differentiate between providers in terms of the quality of legal expertise deployed. Yet on the other hand we are all capable of assessing whether the elements of the service we receive are acceptable. These elements, such as the accessibility of lawyers, the clarity of their communication, their understanding of context, nuance, tolerance to risk, and empathy with the client, etc, are factors we all assess all of the time.

The inevitable conclusion we reach is that value (and therefore profit) will be attributed to the service we receive not to the legal advice itself. Obviously we will expect (perhaps even assume) that the legal content will be good enough and this is perhaps the role for regulators going forward to provide the "kite-mark" of quality we need, but in very many ways what we will increasingly pay for will be the quality of the interaction.

The providers of legal services therefore, especially providers who are not dealing in the high-end consulting services (the mega-deals, the inter-governmental activity etc) but who are working in the broad swathe of corporate, commercial and consumer law must drive down the cost of their "product" while driving up the value of the service. This is something that we can see today in a variety of areas that are not obviously linked.

At one level law firms have become used to pricing the component elements of a transaction or dispute, in effect unbundling their service. This has encouraged a detailed examination of process and procedure that has improved efficiency and has also challenged law firms to consider what elements of a service/process are ones that clients might pay for and those which might have to be priced at a loss, even given away for free.

At another level the claims handling legal services that are provided to the biggest insurance companies focus value on the quality of the management information, the trends analysis and the efficiency improvements. This is as far removed as you can get from the traditional "wig and pen" caricature of lawyers and is in the same space occupied by serious process engineers and logistics management experts.

Moving into the transactional realm, the quality of relationships between lawyer and client still has significant influence. In this area of activity if the client is made to feel valued it will help the lawyer to articulate value. However this is a very vulnerable space which is always likely to be undercut at all times by the latest iteration of process improvement or technological advancement. The only realistic way in which this segment of market activity can be protected is to tie-in the client to a genuinely creative and important value-add proposition.

What does this mean? It means, for example, providing exclusive and insightful thought leadership to clients so that being a client ensures access to relevant and helpful strategic guidance on market/sector trends. Law firms that can leverage their position of privileged access across markets, from regulators, to suppliers and to consumers can draw trends, point to developments and opportunities and so can create competitive value for their clients. Value-add also means supporting the clients' own resources for managing risk more effectively. This might be through training programmes, systems development and/or adding people to the in-house team.

The logical extreme of the approach will see legal content reducing in cost often to a point where it is free, but where the profitability of the supplier is developed through bundled "membership" services, through resource management, access to know-how systems and strategic advisory services.

3. The public sector collaboration

Lawyers who worked in in-house teams twenty years ago were often maligned by lawyers in law firms. They were not "good enough" to cut it in a law firm. Similarly, lawyers in in-house teams in commerce and industry would sometimes look at lawyers in public sector in-house teams and be equally judgemental. Whatever the weakness of the arguments twenty years ago, the position today is very different to that perception.

The public sector is now a major driving force for change in the profession. Major players have emerged who have a dynamic, sometimes controversial profile and the debate on the future of legal services is being shaped by their influence.

Kent County Council is one obvious example of this recent phenomenon, but they are by no means the only player. The opportunity for the public sector to transform itself is partly a natural evolution (taking advantage of technology and know-how management) and partly driven by the necessity to demonstrate value at a time of considerable austerity in the public finances. What Kent County Council have done however, under the strategic leadership of Geoff Wild, is to prove that entrepreneurialism can be harnessed to create value, career opportunities and innovation in even the most conservative of environments.

Now lawyers in the Kent County Council legal department provide services to other public sector bodies both on their own account and in collaboration with a law firm partner. The intention is to do this not just within their geographical/political boundary, but across the country.

Whether Wild succeeds in the longer term in his South East stronghold will depend on any number of factors; his vision however should not be judged just by the results that he achieves for the good people of Kent, but by the release of energy that initiatives like his have unleashed across the public sector.

Legal services in the public sector will be increasingly based on shared resources that combine to form virtual teams that capture and reuse know-how and which join-up people and organisations to make a more efficient, more expert and more relevant service to a broader group of users and consumers

The ambition will be to reduce the bottom line cost of delivery without any adverse impact on quality and a significant outcome of working collaboratively will also be pro-active identification of opportunities to offer new services without incurring additional costs. Done well this will create, encourage, develop and embed multi-functional, cross-agency, real and virtual teams that come together for specific initiatives or which have sufficient common interests that they collaborate on a long term basis.

Public sector lawyers are setting the agenda already with shared panels of external law firms and joint ventures between in-house teams and law firms willing to co-operate to provide legal services both internally and to other agencies. One senses that the extent of change in this sector has only just begun.

4. The integrated solution

Much of the ground explored in this paper so far is also revealed in the final development I want to describe. It is potentially one of the most significant developments in legal services for decades shifting not just the perception of operational effectiveness, but redefining what legal services are and what they mean to clients. The Managed Legal Services (MLS) proposition from Berwin Leighton Paisner (BLP) is game changing.

The proposition came to public prominence when BLP announced a deal with Thames Water. The issues being faced by Thames Water were common to many businesses and the lawyers they employ in their in-house teams. These are issues I see in very many of the teams I work with every day.

- How to manage an increasing demand for quality legal support with capped or reducing budgets?
- How to manage a multi-firm panel for value and build mutually supporting relationships?
- How to create a strategic role that plays to the strengths of the in-house team while demonstrating efficiency in the way significant volumes of operational activity are being managed?
- How to provide a career path to ambitious and talented in-house lawyers in a flat and opportunity constrained structure?

BLP seeing this concluded that offering different pricing arrangements without more was not the answer. They considered that they would have to be more innovative and re-think the way legal services are managed and delivered. In effect BLP concluded that the traditional methods of employing an in-house team and selecting and managing a law firm panel were potentially constraining some aspects of collaboration and innovation.

John Bennett, the partner heading the MLS operation for BLP, recognised these tensions and shortcomings. Encouraged by clients he came forward with a new model. It is a model, underpinned by intelligent multi-sourcing and proprietary information technologies, that is cheaper, better and simpler for the client. The model also supports the transferring members of the in-house team with excellent training, know-how, systems and processes.

Thames Water has transferred their legal team (other than a core retained function) to BLP to resource their legal services requirements with an appropriate blend of lawyers working on-site from the previous in-house regime and expert teams working within BLP and its legal service partners. All are provided by BLP and covered by insurance and extended privilege. In relation to each assignment the tasks are allocated by the BLP on-site management team according to capability, efficiency and the need to achieve guaranteed performance standards.

John Bennett and the MLS team see this as a strategy that can support a great many larger organisations which are significant users of legal services, but I see it having an even wider appeal.

The collaboration has a resonance with many of the points made in this paper and brings together a solution that is client centric, innovative and collaborative. Not every client will want to be so embedded in one law firm, but many will see great value in a partnership which will deliver resourcing flexibility, efficiencies, greater pricing certainty, enhanced legal risk management and systems, processes and resources which enable the lawyers to be more effective.

It is also possible to see the model working for discrete elements of the legal services required by an organisation; so for example for all the employment work or all of the contract work etc. The principle and approach are the same.

Bennett describes MLS as an "optimum solution to maximise value", not a phrase many law firm partners would have been comfortable using ten years ago, but it is hard to argue. Thames Water now have access to as much dedicated legal services supply as they need; lawyers working for Thames Water have great know-how and systems at their fingertips and by combining the former in-house team with the law firm new career opportunities are created for the in-house lawyers as well.

The key to this model's long term success however will be ensuring that this is not a shotgun marriage, but a creative combination of common interests. The work that is done in setting-up the arrangements, with real thoughtfulness and care, will be crucial; but more than that will be a need to thoroughly assess the value of legal services needed and then to focus on delivering and articulating value at every turn.

Bennett describes BLP as being "the manager of value added consulting services" and if ever there was a statement of how far the legal profession has come in recent years that is it. It is the future today.

THE LAWYER CONUNDRUM:
PRO BONO FOR PROSPERITY?

I have had a long and very close relationship with LawWorks, the leading national pro bono charity for solicitors in the UK. It is an organisation I am proud to be associated with and I hope it will develop, grow and thrive in the years to come. I say this up front because I clearly have a partial view, but I should also say that the views in this article are mine and do not represent LawWorks strategy or policy.

It is hard to place pro bono in the modern legal profession.

In the UK legal services are undergoing an extraordinary period of change. Legal process outsourcing, off-shoring, commoditisation and deregulation are all part of this, but so is the rise and rise of technological innovation that is sweeping away old certainties about how clients access legal support and how legal support can be provided. Now, in the aftermath of a global recession, we can also see many law firms in a determined drive for innovation, efficiency and cost saving, but we may also see a new generation of lawyers questioning what they want from a career and certainly whether they want to climb the even more uncertain greasy pole to partnership.

Then consider the influence of the in-house sector growing a role as expert procurers of legal services, the demise of public funding for legal advice, public sector innovation in sourcing and provision and new entrants to the market with niche propositions.

The picture is one of significant and permanent change on all levels, economic, structural, cultural, technological, operational and strategic. It is a quietly irrevocable and quite fundamental revolution.

Is there, in all this, a time and a place for pro bono? And what might that be? These are big questions, because perhaps there isn't a place for it at all.

Pro bono has been accused of sitting in the comfortable higher reaches of the legal profession, largely supported by large and successful law firms where for years and years income has been reasonably secure, competitive forces relatively benign, markets protected and long term planning possible. Individuals and firms who felt strongly could deliver their pro bono work informally or in more organised initiatives.

This market view however has changed and it is not a given any more that the bigger law firms will continue to support an institutionalised view of what pro bono means. Furthermore the sense of pro bono as a national resource has not been realised in any significant way so far. I think it fair to say that it is perceived to be South East centric and also stands accused of being insensitive to the plight of small law firms working in what is left of the publicly funded arena.

So why am I so passionately of the view that pro bono is not just a "nice to have", but is actually fundamental to the longer term health of a profession that is under the most enormous strain at the moment? It is because I believe it goes to the very core of what being a lawyer means and that is going to be a crucial factor for a profession that could easily lose a great deal of its identity.

If a computerised process can run several thousand files at a time; if a call centre in Delhi can answer 80% of the questions a consumer might have about their rights over a defective item recently purchased; if one of the legal publishers can employ more lawyers than the vast majority of most law firms; if non lawyers can part own businesses that offer legal advice and wholly own business that offer "commercial" advice, the question is not what is the point of pro bono, but what is the point of being a lawyer?!

Now we start to drive to the centre of the issue. Lawyers are far more redundant or dispensable in this day and age than ever before; but the conundrum is that lawyers are actually needed far more than ever before.

Before we get carried away therefore by the glitter of process, innovation and talk of ownership models and delivery channels...and before anyone dare utter the damned "Tesco Law" phrase, I want to differentiate between information and insight, between guidance and representation and between access and genuine assistance.

The world does not work perfectly. Fundamental rights are sometimes violated, power can be exceeded and decisions are capable of being badly made. Righting wrongs may have less commercial value to a corporate entity and may be unhelpfully nuanced for a standardised approach. One size fitting all it probably isn't.

In this space we need lawyers; in this space we must have lawyers. Not just clever process managers and slick software, but individuals who are also ethically bound to serve the best interests of their clients. I am very happy to accept that some of this may be work that has to be done at a loss even for free. I am very happy to accept that it will be work that will be deeply unattractive to low margin, highly automated churn machines; but I think it might be the profession's salvation too.

In the end, when we are all wrung out with change, real value will be perceived to vest in those who have a proposition that is not just efficient and cost effective (this will be the least that is expected) but a proposition that is also based on values that resonate; where credibility, trust, certainty and quality are also evident. It will be partly about brand, partly about profile and partly about making real promises of fairness and fair dealing.

In lawyers we will trust, provided they can live up to this standard. What better way therefore for lawyers to demonstrate this commitment, but to have a tangible, visible, serious and long term commitment to pro bono work? Clients can see this and understand what it means; it is a huge indicator of trust, seriousness and values. It is a differentiator in an ultra competitive world.

If you work in one of the great city cathedrals to magic circle legal services, and equally if you work in a cramped office on a high street helping "real" punters, everyone who uses you will understand that a commitment to pro bono sets you apart from the supermarket, the call centre and the generic business adviser. A commitment to pro bono suggests compassion, a values-based service, an ethical framework of substance, a realisation that value sometimes is unrelated to cost, a statement of support of what is right not what is afforded.

I believe clients will be more likely to give their paid-for work to such businesses and I believe the commitment to pro bono is a business development tool that is largely, still, significantly under developed.

Consider then as well the opportunity to engage local communities, to establish the profile of the firm at the very heart of the life and soul of a town. Consider how, for larger law firms, there is an opportunity to deliver on CSR policies in a way that rebuilds people's lives and contributes to a broader ethic. Consider the credibility that is derived by such efforts and which can then be influential in negotiations with government and regulators. Consider the personal development opportunity for staff. It is all significant and all positive

And yet there will be many who still say pro bono is incompatible with publicly funded work. That if lawyers work for free, let them step into the gap left by a dwindling public funding. The answer to that concern will sound glib in the context of a short article, but I believe it to be true.

We all know that a fully-funded legal aid proposition will never materialise (and it probably never existed) so on the one hand pro bono has a role in any event. But being described as a partial sticking plaster is not really the most strategic argument one has ever heard.

The value however of pro bono in this sphere is that it puts a very diverse range of talent together to witness the need, to size the tasks and evaluate solutions. It affords an opportunity to invent, develop and create new models for delivery. In effect utilising the advancements and change described earlier. If lawyers can stay in the space, harness, technology, partner with agencies, develop alternative funding strategies and build out our credibility for efficiency and effectiveness – there will be a way to work and to support this work that will secure a future role for lawyers not undermine it.

Pro bono is not signalling the end of publicly funded work, nor is it incompatible with it. Pro bono may actually be the bridge from the current impossible funding issues to something more creative and secure. A bridge, not an impasse and a way to protect and enhance the role of lawyers for the benefit of all. The challenge for the profession therefore is to make pro bono a genuinely strategic commitment that has a policy role in the justice system. It won't be easy, but it may well be absolutely necessary.

MIND THE SKILLS GAP

I became an in-house lawyer in 1988 having qualified in 1987. Senior colleagues in my law firm thought I had lost my marbles. To précis the sentiment of my former colleagues, if not their actual words, I had taken a soft option that would be less financially rewarding, less intellectually taxing and less valued by my peers...ouch!

In my mind however I had made a different decision. Not for me the slavish adherence to timesheets, or the endless monotony of the due diligence regime, or the greasy pole climbing to partnership. Now I would be integral to the client's strategic thinking, I would live and breathe the client's interests, my advice would be always relevant, timely and useful and I would be part of the solution.

It is certainly true to say that twenty years ago the in-house profession was not really comfortable in its own skin. Many of the questions I wanted to ask only had partial answers: Why should businesses employ lawyers? What was the right shape and size for an in-house team? What was the right mix of work that was done in-house and externally? How should external law firms be engaged for value?

In the second decade of the twenty-first century these questions have more complete answers, but the fact that answers are more complete does not make those answers any easier to implement.

The greatest challenge is probably not strategic. It is, after all, possible to justify most models, structures and approaches most of the time. The biggest challenge is less about process or theory, but more about individual responsibility. Do you have the skills you need to confidently deliver the service that is now required of you?

I am not talking about legal expertise; I am happy to accept that you are well trained, have a good brain and that you know your way around a statute or case report. I believe you know enough law and even when you do not know enough law, I believe you know how to find out more.

What I want to know is can you present well? Do you influence appropriately? How do you build trust in your judgement? Can you manage projects effectively? Do you mentor junior talent? Can you articulate value and are you economically and financially aware? These are the tough questions, because these issues distinguish the lawyers who are technically good from the lawyers who are also appreciated, valued, sought after and trusted. This is the gap that we have to close and the responsibility for closing the gap lies not with the universities, the law schools or with the law firms who train us (although each should do more). The gap lies with us…each of us individually.

The question then is "What can I do to close this gap?" and it is a question I am often posed by lawyers who tell me they do not have lots of budget to spend on themselves. So here are ten personal development ideas you can try that do not require any budget at all:

1. Write a review report: consider writing a report on a specific area of broad interest that will add value to the team as a whole. For example: "With regard to our policies and procedures relating to intellectual property, what are the current strengths, weaknesses, opportunities and threats?" or "With regard to our use of external law firms in Africa, what would be a coherent commissioning strategy for our business?"

2. The presentation of review reports: either to the management team or to the wider legal department or indeed to business colleagues.
3. Work shadowing: junior lawyers to shadow senior lawyers, senior lawyers to shadow executive colleagues. For a day or two the opportunity is to work very closely with someone else and to really get positive insights into how to be a better team member as a result. As a further development point the experience can be written up as a report and/or presented to colleagues.
4. Further develop your presentation skills: chair internal meetings, write and deliver internal training events.
5. Writing skills: write and submit a 1000 word article for publication in the legal press.
6. Influencing skills: organise a networking event for local in-house lawyers in your city/region – consider as a one-off event, but also assess long term viability of a small network that can share best practice ideas.
7. Walk the shop floor: every lawyer should spend some time on the shop floor. Institute a one day a year rule that requires lawyers to set up and participate in their own day on the shop floor (and to report back to colleagues).
8. Peer review: every lawyer to share a small number of files with a colleague who will constructively critique file management, timeliness and ease of understanding.
9. Spend a day in finance: work through a set of management accounts line by line and improve understanding on how the accounts contribute to strategy and business decisions.
10. The 50000 Rand challenge: find a genuine saving (not necessarily in legal) that can demonstrably contribute 50000 Rand to the bottom line. Make a business case for the saving to be made.

I passionately believe that closing the skills gap opens up significant opportunity and builds credibility; I believe it is the only way to assure a career that is personally fulfilling and one which will be valued by your colleagues as well. In 1988 I made a decision I have never regretted, not even for a single day. In 2010 however the challenge is still the same one I had back then. To be the best in-house lawyer I could be was not about how much law I knew, but how well I could use the soft skills to deliver a service that my colleagues would value.

BRIDGING THE GAP

The "bridge" as metaphor has become a familiar part of the communicator's lexicon. We are forever "building bridges" between interest groups and factions and when we note that this is often more difficult than hoped for, it will almost certainly be a "bridge too far". The literal simplicity of the concept and its metaphorical appropriateness are genuinely comfortable side by side and the reader doesn't have to work very hard to see what the author wants to say.

Just sometimes however this familiarity means we slide over it all too easily, barely pausing to contemplate what is actually being described. I am probably guilty of this as well; I can certainly hear myself saying to groups of lawyers, by way of example, that it is down to them now to build bridges across the profession to ensure that clients see real value while also protecting the fine ethical and conduct traditions of a great profession. Nice words perhaps, but I also know that there is a world of difference between writing a well turned sentence for a speech or an article and practically managing a team or business through a period of scrutiny and major change.

So, I would like to work a little harder in this article to describe what I mean and not just rely on a metaphor to camouflage the fact that I have failed to give specific examples of what I mean. What then is the "bridge" I believe has to be built and what do I really want lawyers to do?

First let me describe the issue as I see it from a UK perspective.

In the boom years of the eighties and nineties lawyers

did very well. Work was plentiful, clients were successful and there was a general acceptance that good lawyering would be expensive. Although law firms talked up the fact the market was becoming very competitive, in reality clients did not exploit this and they were not very efficient in the way they selected or managed law firms; in addition most law firms invoiced their clients by one mechanism or another on a time charged basis – a basis that actually rewards inefficiency.

Now, however, the position has changed dramatically. Work is not as plentiful, clients are not as successful and clients also know that every supplier, every adviser and every consultant must be able to describe value for money or risk not being selected. Clients are becoming more efficient and furthermore there is also real (and new) competition in the market from new types of legal services provider and from a number of global players who can commoditise the product and offer price certainty.

In many senses this is mostly good and certainly about time; but not everything about what is new is good; in the same way that not everything about what is old is bad. The challenge for law firms and for lawyers in in-house teams is now probably the most fundamental challenge the profession has faced for decades – how to shape legal services in this century that delivers something appropriate and affordable for clients, but that does not diminish core professional values.

So, having set out the issue, this is where I would like to introduce, I hope legitimately, a "bridge" metaphor; a bridge with many columns relying on a mutually supporting contribution from both sides of the legal profession, in-house and law firm.

It would be very easy to look at the role of the in-house

lawyer and say that primarily they should be forcing down the price of external legal services to their employers while providing through their own resources an expert service of value to their employers as well. In my view however this is misguided. Driving down costs is a legitimate pursuit, but not as an end in itself; at some point we must value quality as well. Neither is it appropriate to imagine that an in-house team can deliver a comprehensive service just through its own resources.

The challenge is huge – law firms and in-house teams working together to deliver a comprehensive service that is appropriately expert, efficiently designed and thoughtfully communicated to ensure value is seen and quality appreciated. This cannot be achieved simply by driving down the price or by insourcing more. Nor, I suggest, can it be achieved by chasing some sort of fashionable elixir for new service providers; they will have much to offer, but not as a comprehensive solution.

No, what is needed is a detailed and open re-examination of what it means to be a lawyer and, in doing so, what legal services should look like going forward. It will be about building a new bridge – a bridge with columns characterised by:

- Mutually supportive relationships that are based on transparency and trust. Both sides must work at this, probably communicating better than they have ever communicated before.
- Work practices that are designed to drive efficiency for the benefit of clients. Can costs be reduced, but profitability preserved? Can risk be shared? Can innovation be rewarded?
- A total lack of arrogance or complacency. The profession faces genuine threat and the old ways will not return.

- A willingness to challenge all assumptions on all sides and to act on constructive criticism. In-house teams have much to learn and must be open to change as well; law firms have a role to play as mentor as well as service provider to help everyone succeed.
- A genuine desire by all to collaborate and to value their different strengths.

These columns must be as relevant to the in-house team as they are to the law firm. For many this will be a cultural shift that will be too much; for most however it is accelerating the already established direction of travel. The bridge is a powerful metaphor to describe the transition our profession must make, but do not let the familiarity of the message disguise the enormity of the tasks ahead. The threats are huge and success is far from assured.

BP - HAPLESS, HOPELESS OR HARD DONE TO?

It is too early for history to judge, but judgements are still being made. Despite the noise and clamour of the moment with commentators and experts at every twist and turn, I wonder whether in ten years time we will look back at what has happened (is happening) in the Gulf of Mexico and see it as a moment of self-realisation for the politicians and corporations that run our world; a time when lessons were learnt and opportunities taken – or will it still be, as it is now, a largely self-justifying, self-serving slick of mediocrity on all sides?

While BP has become a lightning rod for anger and frustration, we are all aware that BP is not actually the devil incarnate. No doubt oil executives from other companies across the world issued emergency instructions to everyone in their businesses in the immediate aftermath of the disaster to demand vigilance and care, the subtext for which was "…there, but for the grace of god, go we; do not let it happen to us"!

The fact that BP is not the devil incarnate provides perhaps a slightly uncomfortable opportunity for all of us to examine this dreadful situation to see what lessons there might be for us as well. I therefore want to focus on what we can take from the BP disaster; so not the macro-economic, the global environmental or the geo-political – but the human lessons on a scale that individuals can assess and consider.

Nor do I want to focus on a lawyer's perspective. Clearly the lawyers are going to have a field day. Claims will be made, battles fought, appeals heard and perhaps prison might follow for some. Again I am less interested in this part of the affair. It is a cliché that the lawyers will do well, but as long as businesses and politicians screw-up we must also accept that lawyers will be needed to sweep up the mess they leave behind. As a lawyer myself I cringe a little at the self-importance of the profession, but I am mostly grateful that we still have men and women of great integrity who will fight for justice. The fact that lawyers will do well from all of this is not a lesson we learn; it is a self evident truth. There are five lessons I want to highlight.

Lesson number one:

Let us not forget that this began with eleven poor souls losing their lives in the most violent and terrifying of ways. Eleven families devastated forever, eleven tragedies to mourn. When we miss this point, we are all diminished. Imagine driving past a road accident and thinking about the inconvenience to our journey, not about the plight of those involved. That would be a sad day for us too.

Lesson number two:

Just because businesses operate on a global scale doesn't mean they are excused from looking after small things. As a young lawyer working in a UK bank I once remarked to an executive colleague "The loan terms and conditions I drafted secured several billions of pounds of assets". In that moment I puffed myself up in a very inelegant way; but luckily for me my executive colleague was on hand to remind me that every day in all our branches seventeen year old clerks would be speaking to our borrowers to let them know that their loan was approved. "They are the important ones, because they are the face of our business and they will make or break our reputation in the dealings they have with our customers."

Lesson number three:

BP at one level at least appears to be accepting that it is responsible for the cost of cleaning up the mess. It is settling claims and has promised to settle claims in future – it did not have to be dragged through the courts, has not tried to wriggle too much and has the means to pay as well. So why is it perceived to have handled things so badly? Partly I believe because it showed precious little humility.

In a restaurant a while ago a very large and even louder gentleman on the table next to me expansively gestured to his nervous looking "girlfriend", in doing so he knocked my arm and caused me to drop the glass of wine I was holding into my lap. I looked up, held up my hands in a gesture that said "For goodness sake look what you are doing", but I didn't actually say a word; before I could saying anything, he took out his wallet, literally threw some money at me and said without a hint of apology, "That will take care of it." He then turned round to continue his dinner.

Lesson number four:

In his resignation statement the Chief Executive for BP says he has been vilified. He is being comforted in this state of vilification by a £1,000,000 pay-off and a pension purportedly worth £600,000 a year. On his watch, his business has caused damage beyond imagining and (reference lesson number one) eleven men are dead. The Chief Executive of BP did not cause these things, but he was paid riches to show stewardship, leadership and to take responsibility.

Taking responsibility is one of life's big lessons. Every day ordinary people do it; they see something and they act on it; small gestures often, but gestures that signify that they are self-aware: standing with a child who has temporarily lost a parent; picking up some broken glass on the pavement; opening a door for someone carrying bags; giving up a seat on a bus. The Chief Executive of BP seems to me to be confusing fault and responsibility. It is not his fault, but it is his responsibility.

Lesson number five:

Was it partly our responsibility too? The Gulf of Mexico is a long way away from my home town and from the petrol station I use every week. Does that distance mean I am shielded from seeing my role in all this as well? I think on balance it does, but I also think we are poorly served by big business and by politicians. If we all lobby for greener fuels (so the argument goes),we will get them; but I am reminded of the quotation attributed to Henry Ford: "... Before the invention of the automobile, if you had asked people what they wanted from transportation they would have said faster horses."

We need to value more our scientists, philosophers and entrepreneurs and to value a little less the accountants, bankers and brokers. We need to value the game-changers, not just those who can sweat assets to deliver shareholder returns.

Is BP hapless, hopeless or hard done to? Let history judge that...however, we can take our lessons now and now is always a very good time to learn.

ETHICS – INNIT?

A very good friend of mine was somewhat nonplussed by an announcement a few years back; he had heard that the Law Society in England & Wales had set up an "Essex Helpline". "What on earth" he opined "did the Law Society think it was doing spending our money on something just for Essex? And what the hell was going on in Essex that they needed their own helpline?"

He was so wound up that I did not have the heart to tell him immediately that it was in fact the "Ethics Helpline"!

Professional ethics, of course, have been part and parcel of the legal profession for hundreds of years; without wanting to sound at all arrogant or self-serving this is one of the great strengths of the profession. Clients, whether they are the humblest of individuals or the mightiest of corporations, can rely on their lawyers acting in their best interests.

Students who come to study the law learn quickly how it is possible to represent even the most reprehensible individual, never to lie or to deceive the courts, but because in the end the strength of a democratic society is judged by ensuring the fairness of the trial and protection from an overbearing State.

Trainee lawyers learn that confidentiality is not just about keeping commercial secrets safe, but a fundamental tenet of their integrity and personal credibility.

Junior lawyers come to understand that privileged advice is not a misnomer; it is indeed a privilege to be able to fearlessly advise a client on their rights, their responsibilities and their plans.

And yet in the second decade of a new century the centuries old traditions look like they might have lost their lustre just a little. I do not mean that the profession is less professional or that access to justice, confidentiality and privilege (etc) are less valued; but I do wonder if it is enough and whether we need to do even more.

In the last ten years we have seen Enron, the near collapse of the banking system, an adrenalin fuelled tech bubble, what many consider to be an illegal war in Iraq, endemic corruption in some States and a legal profession that looks increasingly uncertain as to whether it is a consumer-driven, branded and commoditised service or an independent, bespoke, and hands-off advisory service.

In this last turbulent decade I do not want to pretend that the lawyers could have (should have) done more in a sort of faux heroic role acting as protector of the common good; but I do want to challenge whether the old precepts of professionalism have adapted enough to cope with the demands of 21st Century living, commerce and politics.

It is not just the world that has changed, but the profession has changed too. Look at how many lawyers are now employed by authorities, institutions and businesses to be in-house legal advisors; consider how transformatory the internet and email has been in the way lawyers communicate with their clients and with each other; and reflect as well on how this has also been influential in opening up new markets and new territories.

I see all these things as very positive; the legal profession has become a globalised phenomenon that has, in less than a generation, moved from being seen as Dickensian in its practices to something that influences millions and millions of lives every day by supporting everything from governments and international trade on the one hand, to the lease of the corner shop and a defence lawyer for the arrested shoplifter on the other.

So, given all this change externally and within the profession – should we examine whether what "professionalism" means today is enough? Are we still adequately protecting our fellow citizens? Do we in fact need a new normal for what ethics should mean today? My emphatic answer is that yes we do, but I am not going to pretend to have answers to such complex and important issues as these. I do think however that we need to have the most informed debate we can.

There are two crucial factors as to why we must do so and why there is not a moment to waste.

• First, because our world has changed so much and modernisation does not always go hand in hand with simultaneously developing an up to date ethical code that supports innovation and change;

• Second because in an ultra competitive and de-regulating world where services might in future be provided by all and sundry and where being a fully qualified lawyer might become less and less meaningful, we need to re-assert the values of the profession.

What might the new ethics look like? Perhaps a responsibility not just to see that commercial decisions are made within the tight definition of statute or regulation; but a duty to at least ask the question is this in the interests of council tax-payers, shareholders and employees as well? Or an obligation to ensure that companies and institutions demonstrate a serious, proportionate and competent commitment to regulatory compliance? Or a responsibility to enquire whether the policies and practices of an organisation are environmentally sustainable? Perhaps a requirement to sign-off deals, trading statements and accounts as having been achieved without corruption?

More grandly, should there be a duty on every lawyer to protect the rule of law and to proactively promote access to justice.

I am of course aware that within the confines of such a short article précised ideas can look foolish and crazily simplistic; but at the heart of this concern for what ethics should look like today, is I think a legitimate and very real concern for lawyers. Frankly what is the point of lawyers if all legal knowledge, wisdom and insight is apparently capable of being synthesised to a few bytes of digital information?

For the sake of the profession, I believe lawyers themselves must at least be prepared to explore what being a lawyer means today and therefore to re-establish an ethical code that supports our modern, diverse and multicultural profession. Not just an Essex helpline, but one for all of us to reassert our value and our values in such a busy, crowded and impatient world.

THE LONELINESS OF THE LONG DISTANCE GENERAL COUNSEL

Speak to any General Counsel today and ask them what keeps them awake at night and two things are typically mentioned:

1. The company's businesses decisions are made today on the sophisticated analysis of financial, risk, market and trends metrics – very little of which exists to justify the value of legal services. There is therefore a genuinely pressing need for General Counsel themselves to obtain meaningful data that proves the value of the in-house function, and secondly

2. There is an increasing burden of tasks and activities to manage where the risk of failure is more acute than ever before and yet very many General Counsel are doing so with a static, even reducing, resource.

The two issues are linked to create a further problem.

It is far too common to find General Counsel today spending too much time fighting fires, getting into too much detailed activity and focusing on tasks rather than strategy. In consequence the thoughtful, creative planning and deployment of resources to risk is left to an ad hoc day by day judgement call.

The result is that General Counsel are getting busier and busier but they are also probably becoming less and less effective. At least they are less effective than they could be and need to be.

The sadness in all of this is that unless the cycle is broken, talented well meaning people with great integrity are doomed to be frustrated, less valued than they should be by their colleagues in their businesses and probably burnt out.

It is easy to make emotive points in an article but this is actually a fundamental weakness in the way we organise legal services in the United Kingdom.

A behavioural analysis would suggest that we value crisis management more than we value ultra effective process; that we value doing things ourselves rather than effective delegation; that we mistrust claims that technology will make our work more effective and instead we hark back to halcyon days (which never existed anyway) when our word was taken without demur because it was our word.

And yet in the face of the obvious strain all this causes, I do not believe that senior lawyers are doing enough to change how they work. In my judgement the responsibility for this cannot be put at the door of unthinking chief executives, parsimonious budgets or not having the time to think about change.

The responsibility lies with the General Counsel.

This is now their time to seize the initiative to make sure they give a more effective service, that lawyer colleagues have a better opportunity to show the value they add and that risk and tasks are appropriately prioritised.

A General Counsel today should have a significant grip on the following key indicators of value:

- The relative performance of different lawyers to manage case load, relationships and to proactively pre-empt new issues.
- Effective processes for workflow management that are transparent, accountable and robust.
- Data that supports effective reviews and assessments for personal and team development.
- A commitment to process improvement and personal development.

- Confident budget forecasting and costs management, in advance of writing cheques.
- Knowledge management that is more than "e-alerts" but which is targeted and focused and ensures best practice is learned and embedded in the team.
- Demonstrable value from law firms doing outsourced work, including activity that offers the law firm incentives to become more effective as well.

It has become a cliché to say that one can only manage what one can measure and clichés suffer from being too easy to say. But clichés are clichés because at the heart of the sentiment is truth.

The truth in this case is that "gut feel", "intuition", even "experience" risk imparting a sense of smoke and mirrors rather than analysis. In the absence of data to analyse, conclusions are all too easily distrusted by executive colleagues. The further truth is that many General Counsel have technologies and best practices in place to collect and analyse data from many sources, including invoices from firms, work distribution in their departments, legal risk and even resource gaps to manage that risk. Every other department in the company manages their business using hard data or their management does not survive. Chief executives are now asking General Counsel "how can Legal measure and communicate its value?" Those General Counsel that will survive are answering the questions, while those that will not survive ignore them or worse yet disguise the truth that they simply do not know.

Now, I am not a technology junky. I do not believe, for example, that Blackberries are a panacea (indeed I have some robust views on how the misuse of the ubiquitous gadget has exacerbated many of the problems I describe in this article). So, everything should be seen proportionately but there is some amazingly thoughtful and helpful technology in the marketplace today and at the very least, we owe it to ourselves, our teams and our employers to have reviewed its worth in our own contexts.

With that in mind I would urge that three points are essential to have the clearest view on and for which some investment in process and technology support is near essential:

- What are the team's work priorities and what value do the team add to those issues? How can you identify the things to stop doing and how do you manage the transition from undertaking too much low risk activity and preserve relationships?

- What are the outsource trends (costs, case numbers, effective resolutions/completions)? Can you negotiate with law firms from a position of expert knowledge? Can you challenge their analysis of why things take so long and cost so much? Can you help them find process improvement that will save you money? Can you hook into their professional support resources in a meaningful way?

- What is the cost of the service (internal and external combined) and how is value derived from the mix between work undertaken in-house and outsourced? Do you dread being asked by the CFO why legal expenses always exceed budget? Do you know what it costs to run a case in-house and therefore how much money could be saved by increasing the available internal resource? Are you outsourcing the right work at the right time to maximise the value of your external relationships?

There are some big questions raised in these last three bullet points. Some are daunting and difficult, but they all have a solution and they all should be part of the General Counsel's armoury.

If you are a General Counsel who has read this piece and wondered what to do next, it is not a hopelessly difficult thing to do. At least make time to find out what is out there. Attend seminars, read articles, network with peers and ask how they are solving these same problems. The issues you face are not unique; others have successfully addressed the same issues and in the process discovered that their loneliness is not a fact of life, but rather a consequence of their own inability to devote time and effort toward action.

If you are a General Counsel who has not even had time to read this far…good luck my friend, it's going to get tougher still!

Being a General Counsel today can be a lonely difficult journey, but it can be, should be, the best job in the world. Find the means to leverage your worth and a whole new world will open up for you.

DO LESS, BE VALUED MORE

What is a lawyer anyway? What do they do that means all the baggage that goes with the professional title is worth it? ...The rules of conduct, the regulator, their independence, the training regime and the fees to practice in the name of the qualification?

Is being a lawyer defined by what one does? What one knows? Or how one works? I must admit to being sometimes at a loss to know for sure.

I qualified in February 1987, a solicitor of the Supreme Court of Judicature in England and Wales, a lawyer...And yet the first things I learned to do well involved filling legal aid application forms and doing local authority searches. In both instances I was shown how to do this by our office receptionist.

Although I was absolutely delighted to have qualified and to have a proper job I often went home in the evening wondering if the six years of exams of various types had properly equipped me to assess eligibility on "Green Forms". Surely I should be balancing the scales of justice or at least being a highly paid advisor on some mega corporate deal.

The question I sometimes pose today, as law departments, creak at the seams with the sheer weight of activity they try to undertake is what is the role of the lawyer in the midst of all this volume of work...and how much of it has to be done by lawyers?

We can all observe that nearly everything we do as lawyers involves some element of routine process that repeats every time. Nearly everything has predictable patterns that can be observed and managed without us having to understand what happens before or after. Truth be told, a lot of what we call "legal" work if it were called "general admin" would not look very different.

I also remember the look of terror on the senior partner's face whenever his secretary was on holiday…how on earth would he cope without her when she was the person who actually managed all the property matters. However in the obvious amusement we can take at such a situation there lies a slightly unsettling reality – while all the work we do can be done by us very well, not all of it should be done by us and some of it, probably, should never be done by us.

Not only is it probably more efficient, more cost effective and possibly without greater risk to ensure as much work as possible is not handled directly by lawyers; it is your duty to create the systems and processes to ensure this can happen so that you can therefore focus on what truly matters.

These are five tests that I use to challenge any legal department;

1. What are the ten most regularly occurring, least important activities undertaken by the team? Can you identify them and show their relative worth compared to other things that you must do? Based on analysis of risk, is there then an argument that some of those activities are so unimportant that the consequences of stopping them will hardly be noticed? If that is not the case, is there an argument instead to at least substitute your expensive lawyer time with the time of less expensive employees, suitably trained (obviously) and supported with protocols and process?
2. Also, and fundamentally, what is the irreducible core

role for lawyers in your organisation? What is the activity that you undertake that combines your intimate knowledge of your world, with specialist legal expertise in such a way that the resulting activity, service and results are obviously, and acknowledged to be, value adding?

3. How much time does the department collectively devote to codifying knowledge, improving process and training colleagues? It is important to be able to answer the question and to be able to say, honestly, if doing more of these three things would save time, improve efficiency and save money. Crucially teams must at least have an understanding of the cost of their time; this is not about time recording, but about the awareness of time as a resource…If a lawyer spends one hour a week answering essentially similar points from colleagues, that is probably forty-to-fifty hours a year. If it might take even twenty hours to write a training programme that is backed by a Q&A on the intranet and a downloadable precedent; the investment of twenty hours saves time and money.

4. Are the lawyers equipped with the means to understand how they spend their time? Could tools for analysis of one's activity help guide our use of time, our ability to prioritise and to find efficiency savings? If we had such tools (not, I stress, to record time, but to help us regulate the deployment of our most precious resource) would that not be a very useful tool indeed?

5. And finally, one very predictable consequence for any team that stops doing anything that others have come to rely upon, is that there will be conflict and tensions to manage. So are we equipped with the reporting tools to show trends, savings, costs and value? Do we

have a sense of our true value (see 2. above) so that we can articulate worth and specialness? Can we actually handle, at a basic level, human relationships where people need to be influenced, persuaded, presented to and negotiated with? Do you train for soft skills as well as for legal expertise?

These five tests will reveal a great deal about the effectiveness of a legal team; they will also reveal the extent to which it is possible to transfer some activity away from the hands-on control of lawyers and into the capable and plausible control, of other colleagues, supported and aided by an infrastructure that trains well, checks thoroughly and delivers consistently.

The lawyer's role should be crucial, powerful and empowering; being busy should never be a proper test for effectiveness and value…so, where you can, do less and be valued more.

THE ALCHEMIST

There are few roles in a legal career as rewarding, as stimulating and as varied as being an in-house lawyer. To work at the heart of all meaningful policy, process and strategy within a business or an institution or in the public sector is a privilege and a wonderful opportunity to add value...But not every in-house lawyer fulfils the promise of this great opportunity. So what sets apart a great in-house lawyer from the crowd? And how can you aspire to be such a person?

I believe there are ten characteristics that are exhibited by great in-house lawyers. I base this judgement partly on the experience of working with many hundreds of in-house lawyers over ten years as a consultant to in-house teams and as a commentator on legal services generally, partly on what people now tell me they believe indicates greatness and partly on what the in-house lawyers' own clients and colleagues tell me.

However if you know anything of my work you will also know that there will be no rocket science in the words that follow; no impossible ambition, or secrets to unlock, no magic elixir to have to discover. It is all frankly very straightforward, but in a way this is the essence of greatness; it is something that is within all of us, something that we can recognise for ourselves, but something that we cannot always fulfil.

In this short article I must apologise if the constraints of brevity somewhat belittle the tasks, but I genuinely believe that it is possible for every in-house lawyer to aspire to be considered a great in-house lawyer.

This is not a false promise, but it does rely on a kind

of alchemy; for my ideas are simple constructs that are obvious to all. The challenge for you is whether you can work with them, knowing they are freely available and simple materials and then turn them into something special in your world?

The ten ideas are as follows:

1. Be true to your profession.

A lawyer's duties always transcend the merely commercially expedient; you must live up to the profession's traditions of integrity, honour and incorruptible honesty without ever wearing it as an arrogant badge that identifies your separateness rather than your inclusiveness.

2. Make the simple things simple, make the complicated things simpler still

You are not paid to make this difficult, costly or prolonged. Use your skills to navigate the rocks and the reefs to find the safe but most expeditious route to a satisfactory conclusion. Be valued not for pointing out the issues, but for finding ways to resolve them.

3. Understand your business like no other and be passionate about its place in the world

Your unique value as an in-house lawyer is that no-one combines your knowledge of your business or institution with your expertise; it should ensure that your deep appreciation of the people, policies, processes and politics of your world results in advice and a service that is forensically relevant and supportive. Do this and be passionate about it too because your enthusiasm for what your business does will be infectious and encourage your colleagues to involve you at all the key moments.

4. Keep commitments

Commitments kept build trust. You are not valued for what you know, but for the service you provide, so show energy and direction and allow your colleagues who do not share your technical expertise to instead see value in the way that you work.

5. Treat all issues on their merits and do not have favourites, do not play politics

A very significant author Roger Fisher (who wrote "Getting to Yes" among very many excellent works) once said "never be unconditionally trusting, but always be unconditionally trustworthy".

It is an elegant phrase to describe a difficult concept, but retaining an impartial perspective will help others to build trust and confidence in your judgement and will allow people to come to you with issues without fear that you will make political capital from their discomfort.

6. Focus on genuine priorities

You will always be busy (probably too busy) and may never have the time to do everything that ideally should be done; so you must prioritise and focus on the things that matter the most. Remember always that relationship management is not about pleasing people, but about doing the right things against well managed expectations. To back up your judgement therefore you must also have the means to report your priorities and to be open to the feedback of colleagues who would like to challenge how you have ordered your activities.

7. Know how to pre-empt, influence and persuade

Soft skills like these do not always occur naturally…not as much as we would hope they do anyway; so make sure there is time for your personal development too. Do you have a mentor? Who are your influencers and how can you learn from them? Your success will ultimately depend on your ability to carry people with you and for you to be able to influence the right course to take. These are skills you must practice and hone.

8. Be a teacher not just an oracle

It will always be tempting to be the oracle, the font of all legal wisdom; but the essence of such a role in reality is that it makes you a bottle-neck for your colleagues and is dangerously inefficient as a model for the delivery of legal services. Your challenge is to become a teacher; someone imparting knowledge so that colleagues and process take up the burden of the more routine management of legal risk.

9. Make no assumptions

…Because assumptions are lazy and in the end can be made by anyone. As mentioned already in this article your unique advantage as an in-house lawyer is that you should have access to all key people and information in your organisation. There is therefore no need for you to make any assumptions about anything. In these circumstances as soon as one hears "but I assumed that…" One might as well have heard "I could not be bothered to check"!

10. Present and communicate as if every utterance matters

Being clever and engaged and thoughtful will be important characteristics of any successful in-house lawyer, but being understood is perhaps most important of all. Communication can never be taken for granted...what you say, when you say it, how you say it, who you say it to will all be critical to your success. In the end the prizes go not to who knew the most, but who could impart their ideas most effectively.

So there you have it, the essence of greatness in an in-house lawyer condensed to a few simple points. Ten ideas not one of which is out of reach for any of us; ten ideas that you can mix, match and fold into your way of working...

...Ten ideas to practice your kind of alchemy as you aim to fulfil your potential.

BLESSED ARE THE DEALMAKERS

As the economies of the world limp out of recession, lick their wounds and breathe out a long sigh of relief… what did we learn from the whole dreadful business and what is the shape of the "new normal" for legal services as we enter the new decade? More importantly, right now, do we have the energy left to care?!

It is said that what doesn't kill us provides a learning experience; but deciding what we learn in our professional lives is not always easy to discern. The pace of change is not uniform and this provides a constant conundrum – on the one hand we read of seemingly significant developments like the Legal Services Act in the UK, like the trend to off-shoring, like legal process outsourcing etc…but on the other hand I know that when I wake up tomorrow morning my world will not feel particularly different; the sky will still be grey, the wind will be chilly, my office will be the same size, my spam filter will be full again and the report I promised last week will still be unfinished!

So, as we dust ourselves down and thank our lucky stars that we are still trading, we will ponder the opportunities for progress, for growth and for profit; however do we also ponder how we should be adapting to a new normal of technologically driven client-centric, service-orientated and value-based legal services?

The answer is probably "no we are not" …at least, at best, I suspect the answer is "well, only if we really have to".

And this isn't because we do not buy the intellectual argument…it isn't because we do not believe the world is changing; it is partly because frankly we are daunted by change and partly because we do not know the direction of change that suits us. In these circumstances our natural inclination is not to follow blindly what might be a fad or a dead end, but to stand sceptically still.

My father told me recently, in a heated discussion about climate change…that if it got hotter, he would take off his hat and if it got colder, he would put it on again. I'm not sure that the Copenhagen Treaty negotiators started from first principles such as these, but in one sense at least my father's response is not unreasonable…most of us can only change when we experience a reason to change.

So I am not going to write now (especially now after the last eighteen months) about imperatives or compelling cases; nor am I going to criticise those who believe that their world today is tough enough just now without some Herbert chirping from the safe haven of the boundary's edge that it would be better to play more expansive shots against the demon fast bowler.

My conclusion is that we should not concern ourselves with the apocalyptic, the way forward is more mundane. The way forward is in what we do best.

Can you answer this question honestly? When we are at our very best, what does that look like?

…Because the answer to this question is, in my opinion, the way forward.

Clients are sceptics too…they do not want new-fangled anything and phrases such as "off-shore", "out-source", "commoditised" etc do not intrinsically carry a resonance of quality and value. I firmly believe that what clients want can be described in a very few words: a relationship they trust, with people they respect, where commitments are kept and where value is clear.

To do this you will not necessarily need a JV partner

in Asia, or a virtual office in Silicon Valley, or to manage everything by hard-drive embedded process or "apps" on your phone; but you will always need good people, committed to their work, supportive of their business and above all passionate about their clients' interests.

I have not suddenly turned up the volume on my Luddite tendencies; frankly the world is changing fast and in many respects it is a very good thing too; there is a pressing need to bring risk and transparency to pricing; there is a need to develop multi-disciplinary practices that support client interests, law firms have to leverage know-how better and make their work more accessible...etc, etc, etc. Whether you agree with me or not however does not have to be cause for heated debate...for now none of us is right or wrong on such matters...

By analogy I did not make a conscious decision to resist or to adopt High Definition television or super fast broadband or my children's social networking or the person free checkout at the supermarket or online banking...Each of these things has been absorbed at a time that was right for me, gently, without drama...Some things have taken longer to come to terms with, others not, but the point is that I did not have a philosophical debate about each matter...and progress/change in legal services will be the same for most of us as well...

Ten years ago most businesses would not transact on-line; now clients worry if we do not. We have not got to worry about the next ten years, we have just to live through them and take each aspect of change in our stride.

Of course for the legal services entrepreneurs, for those who want to create new worlds and those who wish to be very different sooner rather than later, there is opportunity for them too...and they will be the catalyst for many things we adopt later on. We have not got to be against them, we have just to realise that as they invent and improve on we have to offer now, then in turn we will have choices to make as a result as well.

Shops do not sell black and white television sets anymore; but shops still sell televisions. What should never happen is that we ban everything but the sale of black and white televisions to protect the manufacturers and retailers of those sets...So it is that legal services will be different in the years to come, but there will still be legal services.

In the meantime, blessed are the dealmakers, the practitioners and the do-ers of today; for now is your time...you are the wealth creators, the employers and the investors of today...and thanks to your efforts today there will be a future for legal services tomorrow that provides new, different and (hopefully) many better opportunities for us all.

DRAUGHTY HALLS AND COLD SHOWERS...THE ALTERNATIVE WAY TO CUSTOMER SATISFACTION

I was standing patiently in line last week waiting for the man in front of me to finish his diatribe. I was waiting to check-out of the hotel I had been staying in...he was not happy to go quietly.

It was a really nice hotel; newly refurbished, all mod-cons, digital this and digital that, 24 hour everything and hot and cold running customer service experiences driven through every "have a nice day" interaction.

The man in front of me however was in no mood to recognise any of this. Apparently at 4:05am he had been woken by the sound of another guest returning rather noisily to their room after a presumably cheerful night out.

He then had the inconvenience of finding that the incompetents behind the scenes had delivered a copy of The Times to his room and not the Daily Mail he had ordered the night before.

The final straw for him was that this morning the "executive lounge" was full to overflowing when he tried to get his complimentary breakfast (despite his elite card carrying status) and instead he was re-directed to the main restaurant...

For all this hardship he now anticipated a grand gesture. I think I heard him say (although obviously I was doing my best not to hear any of it) ..."if you expect me to come here again, I don't expect you to charge me for this bloody awful night".

It is hard to imagine why apparently minor irritations should create such vitriol, but it serves as a counterpoint to something I have noticed about a residential programme we run for in-house lawyers at Queens' College Cambridge.

Queens' College provides perhaps one of the most stunningly beautiful settings for study anywhere in the world. It is jaw-droppingly lovely.

When I first saw the rooms we were able to use for our event I knew we would be creating a unique learning experience that would live long in the memory. But I also knew we might have a bit of a challenge with the accommodation for our delegates.

The accommodation block is the same block used by the students. It is utilitarian, functional, bare, and a number of other similar words that come to mind – like chilly, cramped, draughty, and basic. Showers might be described as intermittent and sometimes cold. One delegate felt they needed to run around under the shower to get wet. There are no TV's in the rooms, no mini bars, no shag-pile carpet...

It is very clean however and charming in its way, but then one runs out of good things to say!

So every event we brace ourselves for critical comments about the accommodation, but the strange thing is that at every event we get nothing negative at all.

Instead delegates and speakers tell us it adds to the uniqueness of the event; that it is really good "fun" to remember what being a student used to be like; that it is nice we are "all mixed in together" and "who needs a TV when the company is this good".

The Old Hall at Queens' College is the centre for our event. It is an inspiring venue, but one which frankly has lousy acoustics and a wicked draught...The delegates and speakers love it however and enjoy every second of being there.

In significant contrast the big city law firms now go to

great lengths to make every aspect of the client environment as perfect as it possibly can be.

One city firm (I hear) has just employed a second biscuit chef!

Surely to goodness I hope someone somewhere did not present a PowerPoint slideshow on the competitive advantage of biscuits…Even so, one knows that somewhere there is a budget and a committee behind it. God save us.

I wonder now whether sometimes we have so mismanaged expectation that we are preoccupied with the wrapping and not the substance. Could it be that we might want to dazzle with the perfection of our environment, but have lost sight of the humanity and soul that is at the heart of every meaningful experience.

After all, we all know that the law is a relationship business, where trust and credibility have to be at the forefront of the desired outcomes.

I am not going to hire or fire a firm for the quality of their biscuits and I am sure no-one ever will. I will even put up with a cold and draughty meeting room, but what is crucial is to feel important, to be part of something where people care, where time is taken to find out what I want and need and to help me get there as effectively as possible.

Lawyers must never trade on the vanity of their architecture, but on the sincerity of their vocation.

Show me a law firm that truly cares for its clients and those clients will never seriously criticise the décor, the absence of free trade coffee or the quality of the freebee pads and pens.

In the end we all want the same things and in the long list of what we want, nice biscuits might not be the dealbreaker.

My ranting man in the line at the hotel would probably

have coped with the Times instead of the Daily Mail, and might not have minded his relocated breakfast, provided he felt people really did care and really were trying to make his stay important. Instead I think he just felt that his experience, despite the trappings of comfort and joy, was that of occupying a soulless twilight zone where the most important fact the hotel staff knew about him was his credit card number...

THE BATTERED SURVIVOR – LESSONS FROM A RECESSION

The weeks have just tumbled by, the months seem to end before they have begun and in a flash the year is nearly gone...This has also been a year of unsurpassed peril for so many businesses - it feels like we have been blown through an imperfect storm. Whatever happened to the charted course we planned in January, just being afloat now feels like a major triumph. I wonder if it will ever be the same again.

From the beginning of the year until now, almost every day has been a journey into the unknown; a journey where the old established certainties have been challenged like never before, but also a time for understanding the true value of the services we provide, what those services mean to us and what they mean to those who use us.

In the space of a short article like this it is all too easy to slip into the glib and the trite, but I do not want to write syrupy platitudes about opportunity and silver linings. The year has been, frankly, bloody tough; and most people still fortunate enough to be running a business are just thankful to have reached this point.

I hope everyone however can find a little time to pause for thought, to reflect on the challenges they have faced (many still to be faced) and that in our reflections it will be possible to take some positives from the fact that we have at least made it to this point.

In this article, through the prism of global recession impacting the biggest and smallest of enterprises, I would like to reflect on some of my learning points; on the issues I have had to confront in my business and in helping others; and on the future as I see it now.

Working through a recession - Ten lessons in life:

1. Your clients need your help more than ever, but they almost certainly have less opportunity to use you; if you can tackle this conundrum successfully it will prove to be the means to secure the relationships you need for the longer term. Be thoughtful, be innovative and be prepared to look at the widest sense of what value means to you.

2. Now you must also be as inventive and thoughtful in the way you manage the costs of your business as you are in the way you try to deliver a service to clients. Save every penny, waste nothing and reward those who find ways to take costs out of a process without compromising its quality.

3. Honesty in communications with your own team was always important, it is now essential. The hardest decision you ever take is to let someone go who has given of their best to your cause. It shakes you to the core and stays with you forever; but it is part of being in business and your whole team (those who go and those who stay) will value your honesty, transparency and integrity in the way these decisions are handled.

4. Cutting back on diversionary activities and focussing on the things that drive income or reduce costs are the only priorities that matter. Do things because they are worth doing and do not waste time chasing vanities. Any activity has a cost, so ensure the investment of your time is properly harnessed to a sense of the return that you assess will follow.

5. Being a good customer to your suppliers is an imperative to help you run your business well. However big or small your operation, some of your suppliers will depend on

you. Be a good customer, manage your payments well, keep your promises and allow relationships that support you to work to their optimum.

6. Giving some time to a cause that matters to you is a renewing experience when the market is so tough. Some of the causes you hold dear (the charities, the initiatives and the issues) in these hard times will struggle and may even fail. Give them some of your time, invest in their needs a little and do not let something precious fall by the wayside that you could have helped survive.

7. Trusting your judgement and driving for change will help you take steps forward when others will stay stuck in old ways of thinking and doing. Change is hard enough to manage, we all know that, but when change is thrust upon us we have to trust our instincts more; taking steps forward down an uncertain path is nearly always better than being paralysed by assessing options.

8. Never cut a corner on a matter where your judgment, professionalism and integrity are intrinsically linked to perceptions of value. Trust is hard won, can be easily lost and if it is lost, it will never be recovered. Whatever the temptation might be to do a job that is less good than your instinct tells you is necessary...please resist.

9. Deliver on your promises; it is now and always was the only sure way to succeed. Now however you must do this so even if it costs you money in the short term. When better times (hopefully) return and more normal levels of activity are resumed, how you behaved in these dreadfully difficult days will speak for you.

10. Plan for your success. Surviving the last twelve months is in itself a significant and important success in its own right. It is probably also fair to surmise that if you have managed to run a business in the last twelve

months with all that has been against you, then you can certainly be successful in a more benign environment. Now therefore is the time to note the lessons you have personally learned and to plan to be a winner in the months and years to come.

As you embark on another potentially treacherous year, I hope the winds of change bring you a safer passage. Bon voyage and take care.

LEAPING FORWARD

"I've got a great idea" said the bright young thing. "It's brilliant in its simplicity, clever in its concept and cannot fail to succeed".

Then the idea died; stopped dead in its tracks, killed by the quiet assassin. It didn't stand a chance.

Who killed it?

We all did.

We who fail to plan how to implement great ideas. Without knowing how to implement our great ideas, what we conceive as greatness is simply and inevitably doomed to a miserable failure.

Great ideas maybe, but all killed by the quiet assassin that is our acquiescence in the shameless failure to plan, deliver and embed that which will make us more effective, more profitable, more expert in what we do.

So, how do we protect ourselves from the heartless attentions of the quiet assassin?

In this article I have set out ten steps to influence the behaviour in ourselves and in others that will help ensure success and six significant actions to take in our planning:

Ten Steps to Influence Behaviour

1. Develop your plans in detail. Focus not just on the "what" but on the "how". Then publish the plans so that they are visible and tangible for all who are involved, but stress that this is an iterative approach, one where contributions are welcomed.
2. Ensure you have thought through the communication strategy. Who needs to be told in advance, who needs

to be influenced, who needs to be informed? What is the ongoing communication plan? How will people know we are making progress or not?

3. Induct everyone in a consistent and detailed way. Everyone involved needs to have the same messages, be informed of the expected behaviours and understand the values that underpin the strategy.

4. Be self-aware of the behaviours you exhibit. Nothing undermines a plan more quickly than not doing oneself what one expects of others. So turn up to meetings on time, stick to the agenda, make actions clear and achievable and always, always do what you say you are going to do.

5. Invest in the appropriate infrastructure and technology to get the job done, but never rely just on kit to get a job done. Emotional intelligence and well managed relationships will equip you more assuredly for the work that must be done than any BlackBerry, Palm Pilot or Six Sigmatised flow diagram.

6. Describe in detail and often what success looks like. Your team has to know what success looks like so that they can celebrate it when you get there. People need to feel a sense of achievement so your plans should ensure that stages of progress are clearly marked and an opportunity is given to note the achievement of reaching those stages.

7. Treat training as a strategic investment. If people need to be trained to help in the planning, get them trained thoroughly and well. Make it important for them and they will respond accordingly; apologise for the inconvenience it will cause them and they will treat it as an inconvenience. And if training is part of the deliverable, ensure people do it, do it well and value it.

8. Assume nothing. What are your contingencies for every significant point of detail? You will obviously plan to deliver the end game but to get there you may need to have thought through how to cope with delay, defection and deflection.
9. Always, always keep the commitments you make. This is the currency of credibility and the means by which momentum is generated and sustained. If you do what you say you will do then those around you will respond in kind. It's not rocket science but it is the rocket fuel for your progress.
10. Be especially cheerful. Project implementation can be thankless, disappointing and bloody hard work...but the positive tone you can set will keep people motivated and on track. A sense of humour does not get the job done but it can unblock tension and generate goodwill...

These last ten points have all been about influencing the right behaviours; the following six points are about the actions to be taken to keep implementation planning on track.

Six Actions to Keep your Implementation on Track

1. Reward good behaviour as soon as it is revealed. A "thank you", a pat on the back, a note to the boss... anything small but valued that will encourage more of what you have observed.
2. Punish poor behaviour, but remember that punishment is not about how you feel; it has to be proportionate to the behaviours observed. If you are having a bad day don't take it out on those around you, but if you see behaviour inconsistent with the values and aims of

the project, note it with the individual concerned and encourage them to do things differently.

3. Implementation is the hardest thing to do in any business. It requires people to work away from their comfort zones to act on trust not on experience. One of the most effective ways to help people through this is to have colleagues buddy each other on key points for them as individuals. For example if one colleague has three actions to complete then their buddy is there to gently encourage and support their fulfilment and vice versa. In this way any discomfiture is contained, support is real and the achievement shared. It is not easy, but much better than leaving people feeling isolated and unsupported.

4. And in a similar vein, try to institutionalise mentoring and coaching. To make the acceptance of change something of a habit, we need to share experience not just know how. Training technical skills may be desirable, but learning from the experience and wisdom of others is far more real and valuable in the midst of a complex change programme.

5. Publish your result...big graphs and diagrams should cover the walls and allow people to visualise their progress and their success. Blue Peter knew a thing or two with its annual Christmas appeal...The "totaliser" concept works because as a species we need to visualise things to understand them. When people suddenly comprehend a complex idea they tend to say "oh, now I see!"...So give people things to see.

6. Celebrate your successes. Small celebrations that mark the completion of an event or stage will galvanise identity around the cause. It is a spur to continue and an acknowledgment that effort has been seen, noted

and valued. This is a powerful influencing factor for motivating people to do more of the same. Leave the same people unrecognised and their energy and enthusiasm will dissipate quickly like water running through a leaky pipe.

When the next bright young thing in your world says "I've got a great idea"...Don't allow the quiet assassin chalk up another victim...

Ten steps to influence behaviour and six actions to support your implementation will help you keep the assassin at bay.

A BRILLIANT NEW INITIATIVE IN DISPUTE RESOLUTION IN THE UNITED KINGDOM: "RPS SOLUTIONS" IS LAUNCHED

I am seeking support for a brand new and I consider absolutely brilliant dispute resolution initiative. The initiative will be launched shortly and will be known as:

"RPS Solutions".

Note the name – it will be game changing.

We have researched the market extensively and RPS Solutions seeks to address the fundamental concerns of consumers of litigation and dispute resolution services. Consumers tell us that price uncertainty, outcome uncertainty, damage to long term relationships, lost management time and opportunity cost all make the current processes and procedures deeply unattractive.

This dreadful state of affairs in undermined even more when one realises that even the strongest case carries what lawyers call "litigation risk".

In other words a claimant can have a near watertight case, nailed on to win, but may still be undone by the vagaries of an unsympathetic judge, a witness delayed on the motorway or an advocate who misses the home-run points.

Lawyers we have spoken to put litigation risk as high as 25%, some even more.

The perfect solution to all this must therefore address as many of these concerns as possible. Our solutions, the RPS Solutions, must be inexpensive, must be quick, must not distract and must provide clarity and certainty.

We guarantee we can deliver all this and this is where RPS Solutions carries so much credibility and has so much to offer.

RPS Solutions will guarantee to deal with any dispute for a fixed fee of £1000 or £2000 depending on the process selected (see footnote below*).

RPS Solutions will guarantee to dispense with any claim with absolutely minimal preparation (and therefore time and cost).

RPS Solutions will furthermore guarantee that any process can be dealt with, literally, in a matter of minutes.

Finally RPS Solutions promises absolute certainty of outcome with a 50% litigation risk. In other words the litigation risk in our model is only 25% more than in current models without any of the downside of those models.

This of course is completely stunning; however we believe there are many more benefits for society at large.

RPS Solutions promises that if its dispute resolution system is adopted then it will literally remove waiting times overnight. From filing the claim to reading the judgement will take, not months or years, but minutes - guaranteed.

No lists therefore also means much less stress for all involved, plus less thrown away costs, greater opportunity to repair broken relationships and more focus on getting back to the day job without the unwelcome distraction of the impending dispute.

In addition, RPS Solutions needs no property, no courtrooms, no offices and no equipment. We will save fortunes on rent, I.T. and staff overheads; savings which can be ploughed back into the system making it available to an even wider audience.

We can also start to attract even more foreign based disputes, adding to the sense of the United Kingdom being the world's courtroom and contributing to the wider economy.

In this regard we have designed the process so that it

does not need any words, pleadings or submissions. There are therefore no language issues and the whole process can be followed without any need for translators or transcribers.

So convinced are we of the value that RPS Solutions that we predict the end of all other forms of dispute resolution as soon as the world sees the significant real and guaranteed benefits that the process brings.

This is potentially huge and it is perhaps a risk to share the concepts so openly, but this idea is impossible not to share. Our timetable to launch is as follows:

- To seek supporters prepared to invest in the concept
- To create the process and publicise it
- To attract our first claimants

We conservatively estimate that we can launch immediately and be up and running immediately after launch.

There is virtually no set up cost – it really is as perfect as it sounds.

Perhaps the one unanswered question you may have is what "RPS" in "RPS Solutions" stands for...

The answer, but please keep this to yourself until we are ready to go live is...

Rock, Paper, Scissors.

Take care. The world may never be the same again...

(Footnote: £1000 for best of three, £2000 for best of five)

Lightning Source UK Ltd.
Milton Keynes UK
UKOW06f0601050216

267768UK00001B/22/P